# Cookies & Cream

## Hundreds of Ways to
## Make the Perfect Ice Cream Sandwich

TESSA ARIAS

RUNNING PRESS
PHILADELPHIA · LONDON

© 2013 by Tessa Arias
Photography © 2013 by Allan Penn

A Hollan Publishing, Inc. Concept
Published by Running Press,
A Member of the Perseus Books Group

Books published by Running Press are available at special discounts for bulk purchases in the
United States by corporations, institutions, and other organizations. For more information, please contact
the Special Markets Department at the Perseus Books Group, 2300 Chestnut Street, Suite 200,
Philadelphia, PA 19103, or call (800) 810-4145, ext. 5000, or e-mail special.markets@perseusbooks.com.

ISBN 978-0-7624-4767-1
Library of Congress Control Number: 2012944543

E-book ISBN 978-0-7624-4830-2

9  8  7  6  5  4  3  2  1
Digit on the right indicates the number of this printing

Cover and interior design by Amanda Richmond
Edited by Jordana Tusman
Typography: Whitney, HT Gelateria, and Mensch

Running Press Book Publishers
2300 Chestnut Street
Philadelphia, PA 19103-4371

Visit us on the web!
www.runningpresscooks.com

*To my family,* for always encouraging me
to do what I love and for never getting tired of dessert.

# Contents

## Chocolate ...74

## Real Dessert ...96

## Fruity ...122

# *Introduction*

**D**AYDREAMING ABOUT ICE CREAM SANDWICHES AUTO-matically makes you reminisce about that sweet tune that came from the ice cream truck as it neared your neighborhood on a hot summer day. You can almost feel those jangling coins burning a hole in your pocket and just begging to be spent on a frosty confection before you walked back to your front porch and scarfed down that ice cream sandwich, melted cream dripping onto your hands and off your lips. Those fun and carefree days are what ice cream sandwiches are all about.

Even if you didn't get a taste of an ice cream sandwich until later in life, you have to admit that there's something very special about this dessert. After all, it's two delicious desserts wrapped in one: cookies and ice cream! These two treats are a match made in frosty heaven because you really get the best of both worlds. The rich creaminess of the ice cream and the chewiness of the cookie are pure bliss, especially when both components are homemade. Not to mention: Ice cream sandwiches are the perfect size for your hand, making them all the more fun to eat and enjoy.

Homemade ice cream sandwiches take a little bit of work and require some equipment and planning, but believe me, they are *so* completely worth it. The ice cream sandwiches in this book are organized into different chapters depending on flavor, ingredients, or theme. From chocolate to vanilla and everything in between, there's something here for everyone. Whether you want to stick with the classics or venture into the realm of sinful indulgence, whether you want something fruity or something festive, I promise you'll find an ice cream sandwich for every occasion.

Each sandwich has a homemade ice cream recipe followed by a cookie recipe. At the end of the cookie recipe are directions for assembling the ice cream and the cookies to make the perfect sandwich. No need to worry if you've never made ice cream or ice cream sandwiches before. I've included plenty of tricks and troubleshooting tips to ensure every batch is beautiful and perfectly delicious. And believe me, one taste of homemade ice cream and you'll never go back to the store-bought kind. I encourage you to have fun and experiment with mixing and matching flavors (pages 43-45), playing with garnishes(page 48), and thinking up ways to decorate your sandwiches creatively (pages 47-51).

I adore sharing recipes and kitchen tips, which is what I do on my blog Handle the Heat (*Handletheheat.com*). As someone with a massive sweet tooth, getting to write an entire cookbook about sweets has been a dream come true. Funnily enough, I disliked ice cream as a young kid and found it too cold and messy. Who would have thought that years later I'd learn to love the stuff? Who would have thought I'd be writing a cookbook about it?

I've spent hours and hours making batches of cookies and ice cream to create the marvelous ice cream sandwiches in this book. My hope is that you'll impress all your friends and family by serving them the most gorgeous and delectable ice cream sandwiches they've ever tasted, and I do hope you will enjoy making them—and eating them!—as much as I have.

# Getting Started

**U**SING THIS BOOK IS EASY, BUT BEFORE YOU GET GOING ON your ice cream sandwich adventures, it's really important that you read the next few chapters. They are filled with useful information that will lead the way to creating scrumptious sandwiches.

One of the best tips I can give you that applies to any recipe is to read the *entire* recipe before you start. We've all been there, standing in the kitchen, following a recipe as we go, only to unexpectedly encounter something like "chill overnight." Reading a recipe completely will ensure a smooth and successful kitchen experience.

The most important thing of all, though, is to have fun with this book! Ice cream sandwiches are the ultimate comfort food and take us back to long and carefree days of childhood. Enjoy every step along the way, and you'll make delightful dessert.

> **A NOTE ABOUT FOOD SAFETY:** In the recipes in this book, eggs are cooked thoroughly, destroying any bacteria that may be present. To further ensure the safety of your food, be sure to wash your hands throughout the cooking and baking processes, especially after touching raw egg. Always make sure your utensils are clean. Additionally, never leave egg-based food products at room temperature for an extended period of time. They should be on ice or stored in the refrigerator.

# EQUIPMENT

The following is a list of kitchen tools that you will need or that will come in handy as you make ice cream sandwiches.

**BAKING SHEETS:** Good baking sheets are completely necessary for baking cookies. I love to use half sheet pans or flat (rimless) baking sheets that are the same size as half sheet pans, which is usually about 13 x 18 inches. Good-quality baking sheets are heavy-duty shiny aluminum (avoid using dark, nonstick bakeware, which can burn the bottoms of cookies) and resist warping. Aluminum is an excellent conductor of heat, which means your cookies will bake more evenly.

**BAKING PANS:** Eight x eight-inch square baking pans and 9 x 13-inch rectangular baking pans are necessary for some of the recipes in this book. Look for the same heavy-duty shiny aluminum bakeware mentioned above.

**BENCH SCRAPER:** A metal or plastic scraper is useful when rolling out cookie dough to help loosen the dough from the work surface. It is also useful for cutting dough, cutting out brownies or blondies, and transferring items from one place to another.

**BLENDER, IMMERSION BLENDER, OR FOOD PROCESSOR:** These small kitchen appliances can typically be used interchangeably and are perfect for pureeing fruits and other mixtures to make smooth and creamy ice creams.

**COOKIE CUTTERS:** These are used with rollout cookie dough recipes. You can use any shape you like, but be sure to adjust the baking times accordingly. Bake longer for larger shapes and less for smaller shapes. Cookie cutters are also used to cut out shapes from sheets of ice cream to make beautifully shaped sandwiches. Avoid plastic cookie cutters and try to use cookie cutters with grips or handles so that it's easier to cut shapes out of the ice cream. If you don't have any cookie cutters, you can also use a glass or lid with sharp edges.

**COOLING RACKS:** Usually made of heavy wire or steel, cooling racks let air circulate around the cookies after baking so they cool more quickly and evenly.

**ICE CREAM MAKER:** One of the most important pieces of equipment in the ice cream sandwich–making process, ice cream makers come in a variety of styles and price points. There are hand-crank ice and rock salt machines, more pricey self-refrigerating machines, and electric machines that require prefreezing. There is even a prefreezing ice cream maker attachment for some stand mixers. For most people, the small (usually

$1^{1}/_{2}$-quart capacity) prefreezing machines are easier to use and more affordable (they are usually between $30 and $100). Use whichever one your family already has or whichever you prefer to purchase; just be sure to follow the manufacturer's instructions. The prefreezing machines require the freezing canister to be frozen in advance, which can take up to twenty-four hours depending on the machine and your freezer.

**KNIVES:** Sharp knives are invaluable to any kitchen for food preparation. A paring knife and a chef's knife will perform almost any chopping task required for the recipes in this book.

**MEASURING SPOONS AND CUPS:** Measuring spoons come in graduated sizes, which should at minimum include: $^{1}/_{4}$ teaspoon, $^{1}/_{2}$ teaspoon, 1 teaspoon, and 1 tablespoon. Stainless-steel measuring spoons are most durable. Dry measuring cups come in graduated sizes that should at minimum include: $^{1}/_{4}$ cup, $^{1}/_{3}$ cup, $^{1}/_{2}$ cup, and 1 cup. Again, stainless-steel measuring cups are most durable. Avoid using 2-cup measuring cups because they can compact ingredients for inaccurate measurements. Do not use dry measuring cups to measure liquid ingredients. Liquid measuring cups, which come in a variety of sizes, are made of glass or clear plastic with measurement markings up the side. Read the measurements at eye-level. I find a 2-cup or larger liquid measuring cup most useful in making ice cream.

**MIXING BOWLS:** Small, medium, and large mixing bowls—preferably two of each—are crucial to almost every step of the ice cream sandwich–making process. Avoid plastic bowls that can retain odors, colors, and fat. Also be sure to have at least one microwave-safe bowl, which is useful for quickly melting ingredients, such as butter and chocolate.

**PARCHMENT PAPER:** Parchment paper is coated with silicone, which makes it nonstick. When parchment is placed on a baking sheet before baking, cookies will release easily when cooked.

Parchment paper is also extremely useful in rolling out cookie dough; it replaces flour by preventing the dough from sticking to your work surface. Clean up is always easier with parchment paper.

**ROLLING PIN:** There are many different types of rolling pins on the market; just be sure to use one you feel comfortable with. You will need a rolling pin for the cutout cookie recipes in this book.

**SAUCEPANS AND SKILLETS:** Necessary for making custard and caramel, toasting nuts, and other tasks, good-quality, heavy-bottomed cookware will heat your food quickly and evenly.

**SCOOPS (FOR COOKIES AND ICE CREAM):** Two kinds of scoops are very useful for making ice cream sandwiches. Spring-loaded scoops are wonderful for making perfectly shaped and even rounds of drop cookie dough. Non-spring-loaded ice cream scoops glide easily through ice cream to make nicely shaped scoops for sandwiches.

**SILICONE BAKING MATS:** These reusable nonstick sheets can replace parchment paper when baking cookies. Nothing sticks to these guys, and they prevent your cookies from browning too much on the bottom.

**SPATULAS:** Long-handled rubber or silicone spatulas are indispensable in the baker's kitchen. Silicone spatulas are even heat resistant. I keep a few different spatulas in small, medium, and large sizes.

**STAND MIXER OR HAND MIXER:** These small kitchen appliances can be used interchangeably and are perfect for baking cookies because they can cream butter with sugar quickly and easily. With an electric mixer, you can have cookie dough ready in a matter of minutes.

**STORAGE CONTAINERS:** Storing ice cream properly is important to prevent the ice cream from gathering ice crystals and becoming hard. The container should be freezer-safe, airtight, and have a 1½-quart capacity. Square or rectangular containers fit better in the freezer. You can store cookies and assembled ice cream sandwiches in reusable glass or plastic containers or zip-top plastic bags.

**STRAINERS:** A fine mesh-strainer is necessary to make custard-based ice cream because it removes any little pieces of cooked egg. Strainers are also useful for sifting flour or cocoa powder.

**THERMOMETER:** Another crucial instrument to the ice cream–making process, an instant-read thermometer measures the temperature of a custard so you will know exactly when it is done cooking. Be sure the probe of the thermometer is submerged in the liquid but is not touching any part of the pan. An oven thermometer is also useful when baking cookies to ensure your oven is heating to the correct temperature.

**WHISKS:** Another indispensable tool in the baker's kitchen, a quality stainless-steel wire whisk will eliminate lumps and combine mixtures quickly.

**WOODEN SPOONS:** A wooden spoon is perfect for stirring custard-based ice cream as it's cooking because it can be used as a gauge for doneness. When the custard is thick enough, it should coat the back of the spoon.

**ZESTERS:** A rasp-style grater is the best for removing fine pieces of zest off of citrus while leaving the bitter white pith behind.

# INGREDIENTS

**AGAVE NECTAR:** Also called agave syrup, this liquid sweetener is made from the same plant that is used to make tequila. It typically comes in three different grades—light, amber, and dark—which vary in flavor and color. I prefer to use light or amber agave nectar in baking. Find it in the supermarket or your local health-food store next to alternative sweeteners or the jams and jellies.

**ALCOHOL:** Some of the ice cream recipes call for the addition of alcohol at the end of the freezing process. All of the ice cream recipes in the Boozy chapter (page 166) use a higher amount of various alcohols to provide flavor. Alcohol, typically vodka, is also added in smaller amounts to other recipes to prevent the ice cream from hardening in the freezer and to keep it smooth and creamy. This is especially useful with fruit ice creams because the water content in the fruit tends to make the ice cream hard. You can also experiment with adding various flavored liqueurs when appropriate.

**ALMOND EXTRACT:** Be sure to use pure almond extract and never imitation. Also be careful not to use more than the recipe calls for, because this stuff is intensely flavored.

**BAKING POWDER:** This leavening agent is fresh if it bubbles when added to hot water. If it doesn't, go buy a new box.

**BAKING SODA:** This leavening agent is fresh if it bubbles when added to vinegar. If it doesn't, go buy new baking soda.

**BALSAMIC VINEGAR:** This uniquely sweet and pungent vinegar pairs beautifully with certain fruits, like strawberries. Balsamic vinegar should be sweet and thick.

**BUTTER:** All of the recipes that call for butter use American standard unsalted butter. There is no industry standard for how much salt is in every pound of salted butter, so you are better off using unsalted butter and controlling the amount of salt in the recipe. Also, since salt is a preservative, salted butter often has a longer shelf life and is less fresh than unsalted butter. Be sure to keep butter well wrapped and stored in the fridge for up to one month and in the freezer for up to six months. Avoid substituting shortening or margarine for any recipe, as it will result in different textures and tastes.

**CHOCOLATE:** *Unsweetened chocolate*, also called *baking chocolate*, is usually equal parts chocolate solids and cocoa butter, with no added sugar. *Bittersweet chocolate* has less sugar than *semisweet chocolate*; *milk chocolate* has the most sugar; and *white chocolate* does not contain chocolate liquor and is often very sweet. Be sure to purchase white chocolate with cocoa butter, among the first ingredients listed. All the recipes in this

book call for the specific chocolate required. Avoid substituting chocolates, and purchase the best-quality chocolate you can, as it can make a big difference in taste and texture. To melt chocolate quickly, chop it up, then place it in a microwave-safe bowl. Microwave in 20-second bursts, stirring between each burst, until melted and smooth. Be careful not to overheat.

**CITRUS:** This includes lemons, oranges, and limes. Several recipes call for the zest of a citrus and/or the juice of a citrus. Be sure to wash the skin of the citrus thoroughly before grating the zest. If you can, use organic citrus to avoid any chemical residue. Also, be sure to grate the zest of a citrus before squeezing the juice. Always use freshly squeezed juice.

**COCOA POWDER:** The recipes in this book call for either *unsweetened cocoa powder* or *unsweetened Dutch-process cocoa powder*. Natural cocoa powder is what is more typical in American recipes and supermarkets. Dutch-process cocoa powder is more common in Europe and is slightly acidic, strongly flavored, and medium brown in color. It has been treated with alkali to neutralize its acidity, soften its flavor, and change its color to an intensely dark and sometimes red-tinged brown color. For baking, it's very important to use the cocoa powder that is called for in the recipe. Dutch-process cocoa powder is more difficult to find in regular supermarkets, however, you can usually purchase it at specialty and gour-met food stores.

**COCONUT:** There are a few different forms of coconut called for in the recipes in this book. *Shredded coconut* adds won-derful texture to baked goods. It comes unsweetened or sweetened. Be sure to use the kind that is called for in the recipe. Shredded coconut is often found in the baking aisle of the supermarket. *Coconut extract*, also called *coconut flavoring*, may be used to amplify the coconut flavor. Coconut extract may be found next to other flavorings and extracts in the

supermarket. *Cream of coconut* is another product called for in this book's recipes. It is often found in cans in the liquor section of the supermarket. *Coconut oil* is also called for in some of the recipes. It can be a fabulous healthy and vegan replace-ment for butter in many baked treats, only imparting a very slight coconut fla-vor. It's found next to other cooking oils in most supermarkets or in gourmet or health-food stores. It's solid yet soft at room temperature and does not require refrigeration.

**CREAM:** Almost all of the ice cream recipes in this book call for heavy cream. Heavy cream contains between 36 and 40 percent milk fat, which is why it has the best flavor and texture among creams. If possible, buy cream that has not been ultra-pasteurized (UHT), because it is nearly flavorless. Since cream is such an integral part of ice cream, buy the best quality you can and don't use substitutions.

**CREAM CHEESE:** Cream cheese imparts a rich, tangy flavor to ice cream and cookie recipes. Avoid using spreadable, whipped, low-fat, or fat-free cream cheese.

**DULCE DE LECHE:** This Latin caramel-like mixture is made from boiling down milk and sugar until a thick, rich, and dark liquid forms. It can be found canned in the Latin section of the supermarket or in specialty and gourmet food stores. Once the container is opened, be sure to refrigerate it.

**EGGS:** All of the recipes call for large eggs. For the best results, do not substitute other sizes. You can use white or brown eggs, but just be sure the package is labeled with Grade AA, which indicates high quality. Since all the recipes in this book cook the eggs to a high enough temperature to kill bacteria, you don't need to worry about purchasing pasteurized egg products.

**ESPRESSO POWDER:** This product imparts a deeply rich coffee flavor with just a small amount. You can find espresso powder in some supermarkets, Italian markets, or in specialty and gourmet food stores.

**FLOUR:** All the recipes use all-purpose flour that is found at any supermarket. I prefer to use unbleached flour.

**FOOD COLORING:** Food coloring is called for in a couple of recipes to impart brilliant and otherwise unachievable color to cookies or ice cream. Gel-paste food coloring is more concentrated than liquid food coloring. Whichever you use, add a little bit at a time until you reach the desired color. You may need more or less than the recipe calls for depending on the type of food coloring and the desired color.

**FRUIT:** Some of the recipes call for various fruits. Try to choose ripe fruits that are in season, if possible. Otherwise, use unsweetened (thawed) frozen fruits, which are often picked and flash frozen at peak freshness. If using frozen fruit, drain the fruit of any extra liquid that may accumulate.

**HONEY:** Honey adds sweet flavor and smooth texture when used in baking. Try using flavorful local varieties available at specialty and gourmet food stores or at your local farmer's market.

**NUTS:** Nuts add lots of flavor and texture, especially to ice cream and cookies. Always be sure your nuts haven't gone rancid before using them. Store nuts in an airtight container in a dark, cool place in your pantry or in the freezer. Toasting nuts adds extra flavor.

**MASCARPONE:** This fresh, thick, and rich Italian cow's milk cheese is one of the main flavors of tiramisu. It can be found next to specialty cheeses in many supermarkets and in specialty and gourmet food stores.

**MILK:** Almost all the ice cream recipes call for whole dairy milk, which imparts a rich taste and creamy texture to the ice cream. Substituting lower-fat milk will result in an icy and less desirable ice cream. A small amount of milk is some-times called for in the cookie recipes to tenderize the cookies and help them spread so they aren't too puffy. You can use any milk for making cookies.

**MINT:** *Peppermint extract* is called for to impart an intense and refreshing minty flavor. Be sure to use pure peppermint extract and not mint extract. *Fresh mint leaves* are also called for in this book. Never substitute dried mint. Mint can be found in the produce section of the supermarket.

**MOLASSES:** A byproduct of sugar production, molasses is a thick, dark, and bitter syrup that is commonly used in gingerbread. Use unsulphured light molasses and avoid using blackstrap molasses.

**PEANUT BUTTER:** Try to use peanut butter that doesn't contain too much sugar, salt, or hydrogenated oils. Peanut butter that is processed with these ingredients is often too sweet and artificial tasting. Using peanut butter that is less processed allows you to control the sweetness and saltiness of the recipe.

**SALT:** Salt is used to bring out the sweetness and other flavors in baked goods. Without salt, even sweet things taste boring. Fine sea salt is a great option for baking.

**SPICES:** Be sure your spices are fresh, which means they should be less than one year old.

**SUGAR:** There are several different types of sugars in this book. *Granulated sugar*, also called *table sugar* or *fine sugar*, is the most common type. *Light brown sugar* and *dark brown sugar* are granulated sugar with molasses added, less added to light brown sugar and more to dark brown sugar. Brown sugars are moist and must be packed into the measuring cup to achieve an accurate measurement.

**YOGURT:** Always use plain yogurt that does not contain added sugar or flavoring, and be sure to use the fat content that is called for in the recipe (i.e., low-fat, fat-free, whole).

**VANILLA BEAN:** Vanilla beans should be plump, moist, flexible, shiny, and fragrant.

**VANILLA EXTRACT:** Always, always, always use real or pure vanilla extract. Never use imitation.

# Making Ice Cream

**H**OMEMADE ICE CREAM IS ABOUT A THOUSAND TIMES better than the stuff you buy at the store. Store-bought ice cream gets a lot of its texture and flavor from artificial ingredients that you probably can't even pronounce. By making your own ice cream, you can control the ingredients so you can make it exactly how you like it. Homemade ice cream is usually fresher and tastier than whatever is in the freezer aisle at the grocery store.

Making ice cream shouldn't be a daunting task. Admittedly, there are several steps involved that require some technique and planning. But if I can do it, you can, too. This chapter will teach you everything you need to know to whip up batches of homemade ice cream that will impress your family and friends.

## MAKING ICE CREAM CUSTARD

Many of the ice cream recipes in this book are French-style or custard-based. This means that you cook your ingredients, including egg yolks, until you have a thick custard before you freeze the mixture in an ice cream maker. Other recipes in this book are Philadelphia-style, meaning that there are no eggs and no cooking. Why French-style? Because this type of ice cream is richer, creamier, and smoother due to the egg yolks and the cooking process. Believe me, the extra work involved in French-style ice cream is *so* worth it.

Many of the Philadelphia-style ice cream recipes in this book—such as Strawberry Cream Cheese Ice Cream (page 99)—get their rich flavor or creamy texture from other ingredients, so they don't need to be custard-based. Generally, Philadelphia-style ice cream is firmer and harder than French-style ice cream. Before you start making any of the ice cream recipes in this book, it's a great idea to familiarize yourself with the details of the ice cream–making process so you'll feel prepared and confident when you're ready to get started.

## For French-Style Ice Cream

1. **PREPARE AN ICE BATH:** This is always the first step to making ice cream custard. Once the custard is done cooking, it must be placed in an ice bath to stop the cooking process and to begin the chilling process. To make an ice bath, simply take a large bowl and fill it about one-third full with ice. Add 1 to 2 cups of cold water, enough so the ice is barely floating. Set a medium-size bowl inside the ice bath and place a fine strainer on top. Position the bath near your stovetop so it's accessible after the custard is done cooking.

2. **HEAT THE INGREDIENTS:** Combine your milk, cream, sugar, and any other ingredients called for in the recipe in a medium saucepan. Place the saucepan over medium heat. Heat this mixture until the sugar is dissolved and it is warm and begins to steam. This will take about 5 minutes, more or less, depending on your stovetop and your cookware.

3. **COMBINE THE YOLKS:** In a separate medium bowl, whisk together the egg yolks and any other ingredients, such as sugar, as called for in the recipe for about 30 seconds to 1 minute. The egg yolks should be smooth and slightly lightened in color after you're done whisking.

4. **TEMPER THE YOLKS:** This step is crucial to making French-style ice cream. This is where it's easy to make mistakes, so be careful. Whisking constantly and carefully (the mixture will be hot), slowly ladle half of the milk mixture from the saucepan into the egg yolks, one ladleful at a time. Never stop whisking. If you need to, remove the saucepan from the heat during this process. This step is important because it gently brings the egg yolks to a higher temperature. If you just poured the egg yolks right into the hot milk in the saucepan, they would scramble. Now that your eggs are warmed, you can gradually pour them back into the saucepan with the remaining half of the milk mixture.

5. **COOK THE CUSTARD:** Now the custard is ready to finish cooking. Stirring gently and constantly with a wooden spoon, cook the custard until it is steaming and is thick enough to coat the back of the spoon, about 5 to 7 minutes. Always check to see if the custard is done with an instant-read thermometer. It should register around 175°F. It's okay if the temperature is slightly below or above 175°F. This process should take about 5 to 7 minutes, depending on your stovetop and cookware. Whatever you do, don't stop stirring the mixture and *don't let it boil*. This ensures you will have a beautiful and smooth custard instead of a lumpy and curdled custard.

6. **GIVE THE CUSTARD AN ICE BATH:** Once your custard has reached 175°F,

immediately and carefully pour it through the fine strainer into the medium bowl set in the prepared ice bath. It is important to get the custard into the ice bath quickly to stop the cooking process. It is also important to strain the custard to get rid of any small bits of egg that may have overcooked. Let the custard sit in the ice bath until it's no longer hot, about 15 to 25 minutes. Frequently stirring the mixture will help it cool.

7. **CHILL THE CUSTARD:** The custard mixture must be thoroughly chilled, about 40°F, before entering the ice cream maker. If it isn't cold enough, you'll have soup instead of ice cream after you've churned it. Cover the surface of the custard with plastic wrap and place it in the refrigerator until it is chilled. This can take about 4 hours; however, it's usually best to chill the custard overnight. The amount of time the custard takes to chill will depend on your refrigerator.

8. **FREEZE THE CUSTARD:** Once the custard mixture is thoroughly chilled, after about 4 to 8 hours, you can put your ice cream maker to work. If your ice cream maker has a freezer bowl that must be frozen in advance, be sure it is completely frozen; otherwise, your ice cream will be a soupy mess. Freeze the ice cream according to the ice cream maker manufacturer's directions, until the ice cream is soft-serve consistency. Note that the ice cream recipes in this book make about 1 to $1\frac{1}{2}$ quarts of ice cream since that is the capacity of many noncommercial ice cream makers.

9. **STORE THE ICE CREAM:** Once the ice cream is churned, place it in an airtight container as specified in the recipe. Try not to eat all of the ice cream right out of the ice cream maker! Freeze the ice cream until it is firm, at least 2 hours (or more, depending on your freezer), before assembling the ice cream sandwiches.

# For Philadelphia-Style Ice Cream

The process for making Philadelphia-style ice cream is much simpler. Combine the ice cream ingredients—usually milk, cream, sugar, and any flavor additions—in a large bowl with an electric mixer until the sugar is dissolved. If necessary, chill the mixture in the refrigerator until it reaches 40°F. Then it's ready to go in the ice cream maker. Follow the French-style directions for freezing and storing the ice cream.

## · · · · · · · · · · · · · · TROUBLESHOOTING · · · · · · · · · · · · · ·

**My ice cream custard turned into a lumpy and curdled mess.**

This can happen if the saucepan is heated too high, so aim for medium heat and never go above that. Curdling can also happen if the egg yolks aren't carefully tempered. Never let the custard boil or get above 180°F because this will cause it to curdle. If your custard curdles into large clumps, it should be discarded.

**I followed the custard-making directions perfectly and still noticed bits of overcooked egg were left behind in the strainer. What gives?**

No matter how careful you are, it's likely small pieces of egg will still become over-cooked. That's why it's so important to strain the mixture!

***My ice cream is still liquid and refuses to freeze in my ice cream maker.***

Was the ice cream custard or mixture thoroughly chilled to 40°F? If your ice cream maker requires prefreezing the ice cream bowl, was it completely frozen before you began churning your ice cream? You may need to turn the temperatures down in your freezer and/or refrigerator to ensure everything is perfectly cold so you have soft-serve consistency ice cream after using the ice cream maker.

***My ice cream turned rock hard after being stored in the freezer.***

Homemade ice cream wasn't churned with commercial equipment and doesn't have the same stabilizers as commercial ice cream. There are a few reasons homemade ice cream can get too hard in the freezer:

• The ice cream wasn't stored in an airtight container with plastic wrap pressed against the surface of the ice cream. The plastic wrap is crucial because it prevents ice crystals from forming on the ice cream.

• Low-fat dairy products were substituted for whole milk or cream. Low-fat dairy products contain more water, which form ice crystals in the freezer and result in hard ice cream. Fat is necessary in ice cream because it prevents the ice crystals from forming.

• The original amount of granulated sugar called for in the recipe was reduced or substituted with something else. Sugar helps make ice cream soft and smooth. If you can't use granulated sugar for whatever reason, try substituting ¾ cup of liquid sweetener, such as honey, for every cup of sugar.

- The freezer may be too cold. Try adjusting the temperature or storing the ice cream in a warmer part of the freezer, such as in the door.

- Try removing the ice cream 5 to 10 minutes before you plan on using it. This should make it softer and ready to scoop.

- If none of these tips work, you may try adding up to 3 tablespoons of alcohol, preferably 40 proof, to your ice cream mixture a few minutes before it's done churning in the ice cream maker. It will help to prevent the ice cream from hardening in the freezer and to keep it smooth and creamy.

**My ice cream is crumbly instead of smooth after being stored in the freezer.**

This can happen if the ice cream mixture is over-churned in the ice cream maker. Follow the manufacturer's directions on how long to churn the ice cream and always be sure to stop churning once the ice cream reaches soft-serve consistency.

# Making Cookies

**M**AKING HOMEMADE COOKIES IS EASY AND FUN. MOST of us have childhood memories of baking batches of cookies with family or friends for a holiday, bake sale, or party, or just to satisfy a sweet craving. Cookies are what I love to bake when I am in the mood for something sweet but don't want to exert too much effort or time. Although cookies are relatively easy, this chapter is full of instructions, tips, and even troubleshooting to ensure every batch of cookies you bake is perfect.

## MAKING DOUGH

Creaming together butter and sugar is the first step for many of the cookie recipes in this book. Combine the butter and sugar(s) in a large bowl and beat with an electric mixer. Creaming builds air bubbles in the dough, which will then expand in the oven. You should beat the butter and sugar for 1 to 2 minutes on medium-high speed until the mixture is well combined and lump-free. Be careful not to overbeat the butter and sugar, or the cookies will spread and flatten too much in the oven.

Now you can add the eggs, one at a time, until they are combined, and add any flavorings or extracts that the recipe calls for. Next, add the dry ingredients, which often include flour, salt, and baking soda and/or baking powder. Always add the dry ingredients gradually on low speed to avoid covering your kitchen and yourself in flour. Lastly, add any chocolate chips, nuts, or other additions with a rubber spatula. It's important not to overwork the dough because this can lead to tough or hard cookies. It's also important to resist the urge to eat all the cookie dough right then and there!

After the dough is made, it may need to be chilled. Recipes will specify if the dough must be chilled. However, if the dough seems way too soft and sticky to shape, you may chill it for 30 minutes.

# SHAPING DOUGH

Shaping the dough is the next step and can vary from recipe to recipe.

## Drop Cookies

These cookies are easier and faster than the rest. They simply require that you scoop even balls of dough onto baking sheets, spaced at least 2 inches apart, and bake. I prefer to use a medium, 2-tablespoon, spring-loaded ice cream scoop to get perfectly even balls of dough. You can make your cookies smaller by using $1\frac{1}{2}$ tablespoon–size scoops, but I find that 2 tablespoon–size scoops make just the right size cookies for ice cream sandwiches. After you've scooped out balls of dough, roll them in between your palms to make them smooth. Then, if the recipe specifies, flatten the dough slightly with the palm of your hand or the bottom of a measuring cup. Many recipes in this book require flattening so the cookies are not too thick for ice cream sandwiches.

If you want to freeze the dough and bake it later, place the dough balls on a baking sheet and freeze until solid, about 30 minutes to 1 hour. Place dough balls in an airtight container and store in the freezer for up to 3 months. Let the dough thaw at room temperature for 10 to 15 minutes before baking.

Drop cookies are not only easy, but they also often have that delightful crisp-at-the-edges-and-chewy-in-the-middle texture.

# Cutout Cookies

These cookies require more work but are absolutely beautiful. The dough for cutout cookies usually needs to be chilled about 1 hour or until firm before it can be shaped. Then the dough is rolled out into even thickness before it can be cut into shapes and baked.

To roll out the dough, place it between two large sheets of parchment paper or plastic wrap. I prefer to use parchment paper on the bottom and plastic wrap on top of the dough so I can see what I'm doing. This way, you don't need to make a mess with flour to roll out the dough. Using a rolling pin, start from the center of the dough and work your way out, decreasing the pressure at the edges of the dough. If the dough is too cold and hard to roll, let it sit at room temperature for 5 to 10 minutes before rolling. Continue to roll out the dough until it reaches the correct thickness as specified by the recipe.

At this point, I like to use a bench scraper or thin spatula to slide underneath the dough in order to loosen it from the parchment paper. This ensures that when you cut out shapes of dough with a cookie cutter, the dough will come up easily and keep its shape. After you've cut out as many shapes of dough as possible and moved them to a baking sheet, reroll the dough scraps into the right thickness and cut out more shapes. Some recipes require you to refrigerate the shapes of dough for a brief period of time before baking to ensure they hold their shape in the oven. Baked cutout cookies freeze particularly well.

## Slice-and-Bake Cookies

Also called icebox cookies, slice-and-bake cookies are perfectly round because the dough is shaped into a log and rounds of dough are sliced off and then baked. The dough is shaped into a log with help from parchment paper, which allows you to manipulate the dough without it sticking everywhere.

Once in a log shape, the dough is chilled in the refrigerator or freezer until firm, or up to 3 months in an airtight container in the freezer if making ahead of time. Freezing makes cutting the dough easy and neat. Slice the dough with a small sharp knife into the thickness indicated in the recipe. If using dough that has been frozen for a long time, let it sit at room temperature for 10 to 15 minutes before slicing. A ruler is a great guide for achieving perfectly even dough rounds.

# BAKING COOKIES

Baking cookies may be the second most exciting part of the whole process, right behind eating them! However, baking is also where things can go wrong if you don't take these few steps first:

- Get to know your oven. Every oven is different. Some run hot; some run cool. If you really want to improve your baking, buy an oven thermometer. Many home ovens are off by 25 to 50 degrees, sometimes more! An oven thermometer will allow you to calibrate your oven. For example, if you notice your oven is 50 degrees hotter than it should be, every time a recipe says to preheat to 350°F, you would preheat to 300°F instead.

- Some ovens also have hot spots, or areas where things tend to bake faster, maybe even burn. If your oven has a hot spot, just remember to rotate your baking pans halfway through the baking time to ensure even heating.

- Always remember to preheat your oven at least 10 minutes before baking to ensure that the oven is at the correct temperature.

- Although it's best to bake one sheet of cookies at a time, baking two sheets at a time is possible. Position your oven racks as close to the center as possible. After the cookies are halfway through baking, switch the positions of the baking sheets and rotate them. This will ensure that all the cookies are baked evenly.

- If you are baking cookies in batches, never bake cookies on a hot pan. If you can't wait for the pan to cool, carefully run it under cool water until it is no longer hot. Hot pans will cause the butter to melt before the cookie dough has even hit the oven, which may result in flat or misshapen cookies.

## COOLING COOKIES

This is perhaps the hardest part of the process because all you want is to take a bite of those scrumptious-smelling homemade cookies! Cooling correctly is crucial, especially for ice cream sandwiches.

Once the cookies are done baking, transfer the baking sheets to cooling racks. Leave the cookies on the sheets to cool for as long as the recipe specifies. Then, using a flat offset spatula, remove the cookies to the cooling racks to cool completely. After the cookies are cooled, place them in the freezer for 1 hour so that they are solid and firm when you assemble your ice cream sandwiches. Some cookies may be assembled at room temperature if they are sturdy enough.

However, many cookies are too delicate and will crack or crumble if you assemble the ice cream sandwiches at room temperature. I like to place a sheet of cookies in the freezer for 1 hour or until they are firm. If I'm not assembling sandwiches immediately, I will place the cookies in airtight containers in the freezer until I'm ready to use them, up to 1 week. This process allows the cookies to freeze without sticking to each other.

# TROUBLESHOOTING

### My cookies spread into flat puddles in the oven.

Were the butter and sugar overbeaten? Remember, you only need to beat for 1 to 2 minutes on medium-high speed.

Was the baking pan coated in too much nonstick cooking spray? This can cause the cookies to spread in the oven.

Was the baking pan hot from baking a previous batch of cookies? Be sure to use room-temperature baking pans.

Was the butter too warm? Unless the recipe indicates otherwise, butter should be room temperature. If the butter is too warm and soft, it can cause the cookies to spread too much in the oven.

Was superfine sugar used instead of granulated sugar? Superfine sugar adds too much moisture to cookie dough and can cause spreading.

### My cookies didn't spread.

Was the amount of butter or other fat in the recipe reduced? Avoid changing the amount of fat in cookie recipes.

Is the oven too cold? Be sure to thoroughly preheat the oven for at least 10 minutes before baking. Also, check the oven temperature with an oven thermometer to ensure it is correct.

Was a dark nonstick baking pan used? This can prevent the cookies from spreading.

Was the dough at room temperature? If the dough is too cold, the cookies won't spread.

### My cookies burned on the bottom.

Was a dark nonstick baking pan used? This can cause the cookies to burn.

Was the baking pan greased with butter? Butter can't withstand high temperatures and will burn.

Was the oven rack positioned too close to the bottom of the oven? The heat element may have caused your cookies to burn.

### My cookies are hard and tough.

Was the dough overmixed? Remember to mix until everything is *just* combined and then stop mixing.

Was the amount of butter or other fat in the recipe reduced? Avoid changing the amount of fat in cookie recipes.

### My cookies didn't bake evenly.

Your oven may have hot spots. Be sure to drop rounds of dough that are evenly sized and to rotate your pans halfway through baking.

# Making Ice Cream Sandwiches

**N**OW COMES THE FUN PART: PUTTING TOGETHER DELEC-table cookies with homemade ice cream to make ice cream sandwiches that everyone will enjoy. This chapter is full of instructions, tips, and tricks for making delicious and beautiful ice cream sandwiches. Hopefully you have resisted temptation and still have some cookies and ice cream left to start assembling.

**A NOTE ABOUT YIELDS:** All the recipes in this book tell you approximately how much ice cream and how many cookies they will make. However, depending on how big or small you make the cookies and how much ice cream you like in your sandwiches, you may have different yields. This may mean you could have leftover cookies and/or ice cream. I'm sure no one will complain about eating these leftovers!

# PREPARING COMPONENTS

Ice cream sandwiches are pretty basic. There's ice cream, and there are cookies (or brownies or blondies). I recommend assembling the sandwiches ahead of time so that they hold their shape and stay beautiful for when you want to serve them. Don't get me wrong: Sandwiching ice cream between two warm cookies is the ultimate form of indulgence. However, this way is very messy and doesn't allow you to serve your sandwiches at the same time.

To make your sandwiches ahead of time, be sure the ice cream has been stored in the freezer for at least a couple of hours before assembling. This way, the ice cream is firm enough to hold its shape but should still be easy enough to manipulate. If your ice cream has hardened too much (see page 28), leave it out at room temperature for 5 to 10 minutes before assembling sandwiches.

I also like to freeze the cookies beforehand. They should be placed in the freezer until they're firm, about 1 hour or up to 1 month. This is especially important for more delicate cookies, so they don't crack or crumble when you sandwich a scoop of ice cream between them. Freezing the cookies also prevents them from getting too soft or soggy from the ice cream.

# ASSEMBLING SANDWICHES

There are different forms of sandwiches in this book, which depends upon what type of cookie is used. You may remember the difference between drop cookies and cutout cookies from the

Making Cookies chapter (page 31). They can require different types of sandwich assembly.

## For Drop Cookies and Slice-and-Bake Cookies

The assembly for drop cookies and slice-and-bake cookies is simple. Take one cookie, place a scoop of ice cream on top, and sandwich with another cookie. Put it in the freezer until it's firm, and then it can be devoured. If making ahead of time, wrap each ice cream sandwich individually in plastic wrap and store in the freezer for up to 1 week.

To make the sandwiches more neat and pretty, I like to lie out a large sheet of plastic wrap on a work surface. Take a scoop of ice cream and place it on one side of the plastic wrap. Stretch the other side of the plastic wrap over the ice cream scoop, and using the bottom of a measuring cup or glass, press down on the scoop of ice cream until it is flattened and matches the diameter of the cookies.

You can use your hands to cup the edges of the round of ice cream to smooth it out. This process allows you to shape the ice cream scoop to perfectly match the cookies without making a huge mess. Place the round of ice cream on a cookie and top with another cookie. Press down slightly before placing the sandwiches in the freezer to firm up.

## For Cutout Cookies

These are a bit more hands on. For some of the cutout cookie recipes in this book, such as Bourbon Shortbread Cookies (page 182), you may use a simple plain round cookie cutter to make the cookies. In this case, following the assembling instructions above for drop cookies will work just fine. But with other cutout cookie recipes, such as the Gingerbread Cookies (page 198) or the Red Velvet Cookies (page 149), you need to shape the ice cream to match the cookie. So how do you form scoops of ice cream in the shape of gingerbread men or hearts? You use the same cookie cutter you used for the cookies.

In order to do so, you must create a sheet of ice cream to cut out shapes with the cookie cutter. This is achieved by storing freshly churned or softened ice cream in a large, flat container. This can be a large rimmed baking pan, such as a 15 x 10-inch or 13 x 9-inch baking pan, or a large, flat storage container. One that has a lid is preferable, especially if you plan on storing the ice cream for longer than a day. Whatever you use, make sure that the sheet of ice cream will be an adequate thickness for ice cream sandwiches.

Keep in mind what kind of cookie cutter you plan on using and be sure the pan will accommodate the cookie cutter and make enough sandwiches. The larger the pan, the thinner the layer of ice cream will be in the sandwich. Also remember that this container must fit in your freezer. You may need to use two smaller baking pans or containers if you have less room in your freezer. Always place a sheet of parchment paper on the bottom of the pan or container and a sheet of plastic wrap on the surface of the ice cream before placing it in the freezer to prevent sticking and freezer burn.

Once the ice cream sheet has firmed up in the pan (this may take less time than when the ice cream is stored in a deeper storage container), it's ready to be cut into shapes and formed into sandwiches. Use the same cookie cutter you used for the cookies to cut out slices of ice cream. I prefer to use tall, stainless-steel cookie cutters because they hold up well to the ice cream. Cut out a shape of ice cream and place it on top of one frozen cookie. Top with another frozen cookie and press down gently until the ice cream begins to meet the edges of the cookies. Place the sandwich in the freezer, repeat with the remaining cookies, and freeze the sandwiches until they are firm.

If making ahead of time, wrap each ice cream sandwich individually in plastic wrap and store in the freezer for up to 1 week. If the sandwiches are to be served that same day and won't be in the freezer for longer than 8 hours, you do not need to wrap them in plastic wrap. If the ice cream sheet begins to melt while you're assembling sandwiches, return the ice cream to the freezer until it is firm again.

# MIX-AND-MATCH

Special care was taken to match the perfect ice cream with the best cookie to create just the right combination, but we also encourage you to get creative and come up with your own ice cream-and-cookie combinations, so we have included two handy directories on the next couple of pages so that you can easily find individual recipes in the book—it will make mixing and matching a cinch!

Be sure to store the ice cream appropriately if mixing and matching. For example, if you have chosen to use a cutout cookie recipe, you should store the selected ice cream in a large, flat container so you can cut out shapes of ice cream to match the cookies when assembling. If you have selected a drop cookie, you should store the ice cream in any freezer-safe $1^1/_2$-quart capacity container that will allow you to scoop the ice cream out for assembling.

# Ice Cream Directory

# Cookies Directory

## ·····STORING ICE CREAM SANDWICHES·····

As mentioned earlier, if you plan on storing the sandwiches in the freezer for longer than a few hours, you will need to wrap the sandwiches in plastic wrap individually. If I know I won't be serving soon, I like to place the sandwiches in the freezer without plastic wrap for about an hour, or until they're firm. Then I'll wrap them individually in plastic wrap and return them to the freezer. This allows the sandwiches to keep their shape while stored. If the sandwiches are wrapped immediately after being assembled, the ice cream may be too soft, and the sandwiches are likely to lose their shape and become messy. Sandwiches can be stored in the freezer for up to 1 week.

## ·····EATING ICE CREAM SANDWICHES·····

This is definitely the best part of all! However, this part may require a little patience. If the ice cream sandwiches have been stored in the freezer for an extended period of time, they will need to sit at room temperature for 5 to 10 minutes to soften slightly before serving. This ensures you won't crack a tooth on a super frozen sandwich!

# Decorating

**I**CE CREAM SANDWICHES ARE A FABULOUS BLANK CANVAS FOR decorating. Depending on the holiday or occasion, you may find that using certain cookie cutters and garnishes helps to add festivity and flair.

## COOKIE CUTTERS

For all the cutout cookie recipes in this book, using various cookie cutter shapes offers a simple and fun way to decorate your sandwiches. Some of the recipes in the book include tips and ideas for fun cookie cutter shapes and decorating ideas. Get creative!

- For birthday parties, cut the cookies into shapes that match the person's interests, the party theme, or even the number that shows how old the person is turning. Pair with his or her favorite ice cream.

- For baby showers, cut the cookies into little bottles or onesies, fill with your favorite ice cream, and roll the edges in blue or pink sprinkles for an adorable snack.

- For Valentine's Day, cut the cookies into heart shapes or lips. Pair with Strawberry Cream Cheese Ice Cream (page 99) or Roasted Strawberry Ice Cream (page 135).

- For patriotic holidays, cut the cookies into stars or shapes that represent your country, and use an ice cream flavor that represents your country's colors. Finally, garnish with festive sprinkles.

• For St. Patrick's Day, use green food coloring and cut the cookies into clover shapes. Pair with Mint Chocolate Chip Ice Cream (page 77) or Chocolate Stout Ice Cream (page 169).

• For Halloween, cut the cookies into bat shapes or witch hats and pair with Candy Corn Ice Cream (page 191).

• For Christmas and Hanukkah, cut the cookies into gingerbread men, Christmas trees, stockings, candy canes, Santas, snowflakes, stars, dreidels, or menorahs.

## GARNISHES

Whether it's sprinkles around the edges of a sandwich or cocoa powder dusted on top, a garnish can really make a sandwich pop. You can find a list of suggested garnishes on the facing page, as well as chocolate and caramel recipes for dipping and topping sandwiches. Chocolate ganache is a luscious and thick topping that can be spooned over any ice cream sandwich, and chocolate dip creates a thin coating that is perfect for dunking sandwiches in. Also included is a recipe for fudge swirl that can be added to your favorite ice cream.

- Dust dark-colored sandwiches with confectioners' sugar and light-colored sandwiches with cocoa powder.
- Dust sandwiches with ground cinnamon.
- Add a dollop of frosting to plain cookies, especially plain white cookies.
- Top the sandwich with chocolate ganache (below).
- Dip or drizzle the sandwiches with melted chocolate or caramel sauce (page 50).

**Roll the edges of the sandwich in:**

- sprinkles
- chopped nuts
- crushed candies
- shredded coconut
- chocolate chips or chunks
- peanut butter chips
- butterscotch chips
- chopped chocolate
- sanding sugar
- crushed pretzels
- crumbled bacon

## CHOCOLATE GANACHE

**MAKES ABOUT 1 CUP**

**8 ounces semisweet chocolate, chopped**
**⅔ cup heavy cream**

Place the chocolate in a medium heatproof bowl. Heat the cream in a small saucepan over medium heat until *just* boiling. Immediately pour the cream over the chopped chocolate. Stir the mixture until the chocolate is melted and smooth. Cool slightly until the ganache is thick and slightly warm to the touch, but still pourable. The ganache can be stored in an airtight container in the refrigerator for up to 2 weeks. Let it come to room temperature before using.

## CHOCOLATE DIP

**MAKES ABOUT 1 CUP**

**8 ounces semisweet chocolate, chopped**
**3 tablespoons vegetable oil**

Place the chocolate and oil in a microwave-safe bowl and microwave in 20-second bursts, stirring between each burst, until melted and smooth. Cool until just warm. The dip can be stored in an airtight container in the refrigerator for up to 2 weeks. Let it come to room temperature before using.

## SALTED CARAMEL SAUCE

**MAKES ABOUT 1¼ CUPS**

**1 cup granulated sugar**
**½ cup plus 1 tablespoon heavy cream**
**5 tablespoons unsalted butter**
**1 teaspoon Fleur de Sel or gray sea salt**

In a medium dry saucepan, cook the sugar over medium heat, swirling the pot occasionally, until the sugar melts and begins to turn a deep golden color, about 5 to 6 minutes. Turn off the heat and *carefully* add the cream and then the butter to the pot, whisking constantly, until the mixture is smooth.

The caramel may seize but will melt as it's heated. Add the salt. Transfer the caramel to a small container and let cool until at room temperature. The caramel can be stored in an airtight container in the refrigerator for up to 2 weeks. Let it come to room temperature before using.

## FUDGE SWIRL

**MAKES ABOUT 2 CUPS**

**¾ cup heavy cream**
**2 tablespoons unsalted butter**
**½ cup granulated sugar**
**¼ cup packed light brown sugar**
**1 cup (6 ounces) semisweet or bittersweet chocolate chips**
**Pinch of fine sea salt**
**1 teaspoon vanilla extract**

Heat the cream, butter, granulated sugar, and brown sugar in a small saucepan over low heat. Bring the mixture just to a boil and cook until sugar dissolves, about 2 to 3 minutes. Remove from heat and stir in the chocolate chips. Let the mixture stand for 4 to 5 minutes before stirring until completely smooth. Stir in the salt and vanilla.

Let the mixture cool to room temperature. Fudge Swirl can be stored in an airtight container in the refrigerator for up to 2 days. Bring to room temperature before using.

## MORE IDEAS

If you're making sandwiches that you plan on serving to guests, making sure they are visually pleasing can be almost as important as how they taste—and they'll definitely be sure to impress. To give your sandwiches that extra special something, try some of these ideas:

• Wrap ice cream sandwiches in pieces of parchment paper or decorative paper to serve.

• Tie ribbons, twine, or raffia around the ice cream sandwiches.

• Insert popsicle sticks into the ice cream to make ice cream sandwich pops.

• Use colorful food decorating gel pens found in the baking aisle of the grocery store to accent cookie cutter shapes or to create faces or letters on the cookies.

• Combine two small scoops of different ice creams, such as Double Chocolate Ice Cream (page 94) and Roasted Strawberry Ice Cream (page 135), to make a colorful multiflavored sandwich.

• Use miniature cookie cutters to cut out small inserts in the center of any cutout cookie for a peek-a-boo effect.

# Classics

**THIS CHAPTER IS FILLED WITH TRIED-AND-TRUE FAVORITES THAT** we all grew up eating and loving. I remember back in grade school, one of the best parts of the day was at lunch, when I could buy a cookie for a quarter. No matter how questionable the meat of the day was, that cookie was always such a sweet treat to enjoy. The recipes in this chapter pay homage to those favorite cookies and ice creams that have stayed with us through adulthood.

If your kitchen suddenly smells like grandma's house or the bakery down the street from your childhood neighborhood, you know you're doing something right. Who doesn't love biting into a homemade chocolate chip cookie? Or opening the freezer to find an all-time favorite ice cream? There's nothing better than the simple joy of biting into a homemade treat.

# Classic Ice Cream Sandwich

*This is the traditional sandwich that comes to mind when most people think about ice cream sandwiches. Unlike the typically bland and soggy sandwiches you buy at the store, this recipe creates a rich and flavorful vanilla ice cream with a chewy and fudgelike chocolate wafer cookie that is sure to delight any sweet tooth.*

## FRENCH VANILLA ICE CREAM

**MAKES ABOUT 1 QUART**

**1½ cups whole milk**

**1½ cups heavy cream**

**¾ cup granulated sugar, divided**

**¼ teaspoon fine sea salt**

**1 vanilla bean, split in half lengthwise and seeded**

**4 large egg yolks**

Prepare an ice bath by filling a large bowl with ice cubes and 1 to 2 cups of water. Place a medium bowl fitted with a fine strainer inside the ice bath.

In a medium saucepan, combine the milk, cream, ½ cup sugar, salt, and the seeds and pod from the vanilla bean. Set over medium heat, stirring occasionally, until the mixture is warm and begins to steam, about 5 minutes.

In a medium bowl, whisk together the egg yolks and the remaining ¼ cup sugar. Carefully whisk half of the warm milk mixture into the egg yolks, one ladleful at a time, until the egg mixture is warmed. Whisk the egg-milk mixture back into the saucepan. Cook the mixture over medium heat, stirring constantly with a wooden spoon, until it is thick enough to coat the back of the spoon and registers around 175°F on an instant-read thermometer, about 5 to 7 minutes. Be careful not to boil the mixture.

Immediately strain the mixture through the fine strainer into the prepared ice bath. Discard the vanilla bean pod. Cool the custard in the ice bath until it reaches room temperature, stirring often. Press plastic wrap against the surface of the custard and refrigerate until chilled, about 4 hours or up to 1 day.

Pour the chilled mixture into an ice cream maker and freeze according to the manufacturer's directions. Transfer the ice cream to a large rimmed baking sheet or other flat container, spreading evenly. Cover the ice cream surface with plastic wrap and freeze until the ice cream is firm, at least 2 hours.

> *Tip:* Don't toss the leftover bean pod. Mix it in with 2 cups of sugar in an airtight container and let it sit for 1 to 2 weeks—and you've got vanilla sugar! Use it when making pancakes, waffles, muffins, cocoa, coffee, or give it as a gift to your friends and family.

## CHOCOLATE WAFER COOKIES

**MAKES ABOUT 20 SQUARE COOKIES**

**2¹/₂ cups all-purpose flour**

**¹/₂ cup unsweetened Dutch-process cocoa powder**

**2¹/₂ teaspoons baking powder**

**¹/₄ teaspoon fine sea salt**

**6 ounces (1¹/₂ sticks) unsalted butter, at room temperature**

**1¹/₂ cups granulated sugar**

**2 large eggs**

**2 teaspoons pure vanilla extract**

**1 tablespoon milk**

In a medium bowl, sift together the flour, cocoa powder, baking powder, and salt.

In a large bowl, use an electric mixer to beat the butter and sugar on medium-high speed until smooth and well combined, 1 to 2 minutes. Add the eggs, one at a time, until well combined. Add the vanilla extract and milk. On low speed, gradually add the flour mixture and beat until thoroughly combined.

Shape the dough into a flat disk and wrap in plastic. Chill in the refrigerator until firm, about 1 hour or up to 2 days.

Line large baking sheets with parchment paper or silicone baking mats. Place the chilled dough in between two large pieces of parchment paper or plastic wrap on a work surface. Roll the dough out to a ¹/₄-inch thickness, using the parchment paper to prevent sticking. If the dough is too firm, let it sit at room temperature for 5 to 10 minutes before rolling. Use a 3-inch square cookie cutter to cut out squares from the dough and place on prepared baking sheets, spreading at least a ¹/₂ inch apart. Reroll remaining scraps of dough to a ¹/₄-inch thickness, cut out more squares, and place on prepared baking sheets.

Chill the baking sheets in the refrigerator for 30 minutes, or until the dough squares are firm.

Preheat the oven to 350°F.

Remove the baking sheets from the refrigerator and prick the dough squares all over with the probe of an instant-read thermometer or the blunt end of a skewer or chopstick. Bake for 10 to 11 minutes, or until the cookies are set. Let cool on baking sheets for 5 minutes before removing to a wire rack to cool completely. Freeze the cookies until frozen, at least 1 hour. Cookies can be stored in airtight containers in the freezer for up to 1 month.

**TO ASSEMBLE,** remove the ice cream sheet from the freezer. Using the same cookie cutter, cut out a square of ice cream and sandwich it between two cookies. Repeat for the remaining cookies, working quickly. If the ice cream begins to melt, return it to the freezer until it is firm again. Freeze the sandwiches until firm, at least 1 hour, before serving.

*Tip:* The probe of an instant-read thermometer or the blunt end of a skewer works best to create those big, round holes in the cookies that look just like the ice cream sandwiches you probably grew up eating. If you don't have either of these, you can also use a fork or toothpick.

# Chocolate Chip Ice Cream Sandwich

*Who doesn't love Chocolate Chip Cookies? This sandwich marries the slight butterscotch flavor of these chewy cookies with scrumptious Butterscotch Ice Cream for a match made in heaven. Your friends and family will love these amazing ice cream sandwiches!*

## BUTTERSCOTCH ICE CREAM

### MAKES ABOUT 1 QUART

**2 tablespoons unsalted butter**
**1 cup packed light brown sugar**
**1 tablespoon vanilla extract**
**2 cups heavy cream, divided**
**1½ cups whole milk**
**¼ teaspoon fine sea salt**
**4 large egg yolks**

In a medium saucepan set over medium heat, melt the butter. Add the sugar and vanilla and stir until the sugar is dissolved and the mixture begins to bubble, about 3 to 4 minutes. Add a ½ cup of the heavy cream, whisking until smooth. Remove the butterscotch from the heat and allow to cool while making the ice cream.

Prepare an ice bath by filling a large bowl with ice cubes and 1 to 2 cups of water. Place a medium bowl fitted with a fine strainer inside the ice bath.

In a medium saucepan, combine the milk, remaining 1½ cups cream, and salt. Set over medium heat, stirring occasionally, until the mixture is warm and begins to steam, about 5 minutes.

In a medium bowl, whisk the egg yolks until smooth. Whisk half of the warm milk mixture into the egg yolks, one ladleful at a time, until the egg mixture is warmed and smooth. Pour the egg-milk mixture back into the saucepan. Cook the mixture over medium heat, stirring constantly with a wooden spoon, until it is thick enough to coat the back of the spoon and registers around 175°F on an instant-read thermometer, about 5 minutes. Be careful not to boil.

Immediately strain the mixture through the fine strainer into the prepared ice bath. Add the butterscotch to the ice cream custard, stirring to combine. Cool the custard in the ice

bath until room temperature, stirring often. Press plastic wrap against the surface of the custard and refrigerate until chilled, about 4 hours or up to 1 day.

Pour the chilled mixture into an ice cream maker and freeze according to the manufacturer's directions. Transfer the ice cream to an airtight container, press plastic wrap against the ice cream surface, and freeze until it is firm and the flavor is ripened, at least 2 hours.

# CHOCOLATE CHIP COOKIES

**MAKES ABOUT 18 COOKIES**

1³/₄ **cups all-purpose flour**
½ **teaspoon baking soda**
½ **teaspoon baking powder**
¼ **teaspoon fine sea salt**
4 **ounces (1 stick) unsalted butter, at room temperature**
½ **cup granulated sugar**
½ **cup packed light brown sugar**
1 **large egg**
1 **tablespoon milk**
2 **teaspoons vanilla extract**
1 **cup semisweet chocolate chips**

Preheat the oven to 350°F. Line baking sheets with parchment paper or silicone baking mats.

In a medium bowl, whisk together the flour, baking soda, baking powder, and salt.

In a large bowl, use an electric mixer to beat the butter and sugars on medium-high speed until well combined and smooth, about 1 to 2 minutes. Beat in the egg, milk, and vanilla. On low speed, gradually add the flour mixture and beat until combined. Fold in the semisweet chocolate chips with a rubber spatula.

Using a spoon or spring-loaded scoop, drop 2 tablespoon–sized balls of dough onto prepared baking sheets. Flatten slightly with the palm of your hand.

Bake for about 10 to 12 minutes, or until the edges are slightly browned. Let cool on the baking sheets for 5 minutes before removing to wire racks to cool completely. Freeze the cookies until frozen, at least 1 hour. Cookies can be stored in airtight containers in the freezer for up to 1 month.

## For Decorating:

**Miniature chocolate chips (about 1 cup), for rolling**

**TO ASSEMBLE,** top one cookie with a scoop of ice cream. Place another cookie on top of the ice cream and gently press down to form a sandwich. Roll the edges in the chocolate chips. Immediately place the sandwich in the freezer. Freeze for at least 2 hours before serving.

# Snickerdoodle Ice Cream Sandwich

*Comforting Cinnamon Ice Cream and soft Sugar Cookies combine to create that fun snickerdoo-dle flavor you probably loved as a kid. These sandwiches are perfect for a balmy summer after-noon, during the holidays, or any time in between.*

## CINNAMON ICE CREAM

### MAKES ABOUT 1 QUART

1¹⁄₂ cups whole milk
1¹⁄₂ cups heavy cream
³⁄₄ cup granulated sugar, divided
¹⁄₄ teaspoon fine sea salt
2 teaspoons ground cinnamon
1 teaspoon vanilla extract
4 large egg yolks

Prepare an ice bath by filling a large bowl with ice cubes and 1 to 2 cups of water. Place a medium bowl fitted with a fine strainer inside the ice bath.

In a medium saucepan, combine the milk, cream, ¹⁄₂ cup sugar, salt, cinnamon, and vanilla. Set over medium heat, stirring occa-sionally, until the mixture is warm and begins to steam, about 5 minutes.

In a medium bowl, whisk together the egg yolks and the remaining ¹⁄₄ cup sugar. Carefully whisk half of the warm milk mixture into the egg yolks, one ladleful at a time, until the egg mixture is warmed. Whisk the egg-milk mix-ture back into the saucepan. Cook the mixture over medium heat, stirring constantly with a wooden spoon, until the mixture is thick enough to coat the back of the spoon and reg-isters around 175°F on an instant-read ther-mometer, about 5 to 7 minutes. Be careful not to boil the mixture.

Immediately strain the mixture through the fine strainer into the prepared ice bath. Cool the custard in the ice bath until it reaches room temperature, stirring often. Press plastic wrap against the surface of the custard and refriger-ate until chilled, about 4 hours or up to 1 day.

Pour the chilled mixture into an ice cream maker and freeze according to the manufac-

turer's directions. Transfer the ice cream to an airtight container, press plastic wrap against the ice cream surface, and freeze until it is firm and the flavor is ripened, at least 2 hours.

## SUGAR COOKIES

**MAKES ABOUT 20 COOKIES**

- 1³/₄ **cups all-purpose flour**
- ¹/₂ **teaspoon baking powder**
- ¹/₄ **teaspoon baking soda**
- ¹/₄ **teaspoon fine sea salt**
- 4 **ounces (1 stick) unsalted butter, at room temperature**
- 2 **ounces cream cheese, at room temperature**
- 1 **cup granulated sugar, divided**
- 1 **large egg**
- 1 **teaspoon vanilla extract**

Preheat the oven to 350°F. Line large baking sheets with parchment paper or silicone baking mats.

In a medium bowl, whisk together the flour, baking powder, baking soda, and salt to combine.

In a large bowl, use an electric mixer to beat the butter, cream cheese, and ³/₄ cup sugar on medium-high speed until well combined and smooth, about 3 minutes. Add the egg and vanilla and beat until combined. On low speed, slowly add the flour mixture and beat until combined.

Place the remaining ¹/₄ cup sugar in a shallow dish. Roll the dough into 2 tablespoon–sized balls, then roll in the sugar to coat evenly. Place the dough balls on the prepared baking sheets and flatten with the bottom of a measuring cup or glass.

Bake for 10 to 12 minutes, or until the cookies are set and begin to brown. Let the cookies cool for 5 minutes before removing to a wire rack to cool completely. Freeze the cookies until firm, at least 1 hour. The cookies can be stored in airtight containers in the freezer for up to 1 month.

### *For Decorating:*

**Ground cinnamon, for garnish (optional)**

**TO ASSEMBLE,** top one cookie with a scoop of ice cream. Place another cookie on top of the ice cream and gently press down to form a sandwich. Sprinkle the sandwich with a pinch of ground cinnamon, if desired. Immediately place the sandwich in the freezer. Repeat for the remaining cookies. Freeze for at least 2 hours before serving.

# Rocky Road Ice Cream Sandwich

*It is said that rocky road ice cream was invented during the Great Depression to make people smile. This ice cream sandwich, which combines sweet and nutty Almond Ice Cream with soft and fun Marshmallow-Studded Chocolate Cookies, is sure to make you smile.*

## ALMOND ICE CREAM

**MAKES ABOUT 1 QUART**

1½ **cups whole milk**
1½ **cups heavy cream**
¾ **cup granulated sugar, divided**
¼ **teaspoon fine sea salt**
4 **large egg yolks**
1 **teaspoon almond extract**
¼ **teaspoon vanilla extract**
⅔ **cup toasted slivered almonds, chopped**

Prepare an ice bath by filling a large bowl with ice cubes and 1 to 2 cups of water. Place a medium bowl fitted with a fine strainer inside the ice bath.

In a medium saucepan, combine the milk, cream, ½ cup sugar, and salt. Set over medium heat, stirring occasionally, until the mixture is warm and begins to steam, about 5 minutes.

In a medium bowl, whisk together the egg yolks and the remaining ¼ cup sugar. Carefully whisk half of the warm milk mixture into the egg yolks, one ladleful at a time, until the egg mixture is warmed. Whisk the egg-milk mixture back into the saucepan. Cook the mixture over medium heat, stirring constantly with a wooden spoon, until it is thick enough to coat the back of the spoon and registers around 175°F on an instant-read thermometer, about 5 to 7 minutes. Be careful not to boil the mixture.

Immediately strain the mixture through the fine strainer into the prepared ice bath. Stir in the almond and vanilla extracts. Cool the custard in the ice bath until it reaches room temperature, stirring often. Press plastic wrap against the surface of the custard and refrigerate until chilled, about 4 hours or up to 1 day.

Pour the chilled mixture into an ice cream maker. Freeze according to the manufacturer's directions. During the last minutes of churning, add the almonds to the ice cream and churn

until thoroughly combined. Transfer the ice cream to an airtight container, press plastic wrap against the ice cream's surface, and freeze until firm and the flavor is ripened, at least 2 hours.

## MARSHMALLOW-STUDDED CHOCOLATE COOKIES

**MAKES ABOUT 18 COOKIES**

1¼ **cups all-purpose flour**
¾ **cup unsweetened Dutch-process cocoa powder**
½ **teaspoon baking soda**
¼ **teaspoon fine sea salt**
4 **ounces (1 stick) unsalted butter, at room temperature**
½ **cup granulated sugar**
½ **cup packed light brown sugar**
1 **large egg**
1 **tablespoon milk**
1 **teaspoon vanilla extract**
½ **cup semisweet chocolate chips**
¾ **cup miniature marshmallows**

Preheat the oven to 350°F. Line baking sheets with parchment paper or silicone baking mats.

In a medium bowl, sift together the flour, cocoa powder, baking soda, and salt.

In a large bowl, use an electric mixer to beat the butter and sugars on medium-high speed until well combined and smooth. Beat in the egg, milk, and vanilla. On low speed, gradually add the flour mixture and beat until combined. Fold in the chocolate chips with a rubber spatula.

Using a spoon or spring-loaded scoop, drop 2 tablespoon–sized balls of dough onto prepared baking sheets. Flatten slightly with the palm of your hand. Bake for 8 minutes.

Remove the baking sheets from the oven and press four marshmallows into each cookie. Bake for an additional 3 to 4 minutes, or until the cookies are set and the marshmallows are slightly puffed. Let cool on baking sheets for 10 minutes before removing to wire racks to cool completely. Freeze the cookies until firm, at least 1 hour. The cookies can be stored in airtight containers in the freezer for up to 1 month.

**TO ASSEMBLE,** top one cookie with a scoop of ice cream. Place another cookie on top of the ice cream and gently press down to form a sandwich. Immediately place the sandwich in the freezer. Repeat for the remaining cookies. Freeze for at least 1 hour before serving.

# White Chocolate Macadamia Nut Sandwich

*This ice cream sandwich takes a traditional flavor combination—white chocolate and macadamia nuts—and amps up the volume with two small but key ingredients. A touch of orange zest and a pinch of sea salt will leave you craving this sandwich for days.*

## WHITE CHOCOLATE ICE CREAM

### MAKES ABOUT 1 QUART

1 1/2 **cups whole milk**
1 1/2 **cups heavy cream**
1/2 **cup granulated sugar**
1/4 **teaspoon fine sea salt**
1/2 **teaspoon vanilla extract**
6 **ounces white chocolate, melted**
4 **large egg yolks**
1/2 **teaspoon orange zest**

Prepare an ice bath by filling a large bowl with ice cubes and 1 to 2 cups of water. Place a medium bowl fitted with a fine strainer inside the ice bath.

In a medium saucepan, combine the milk, cream, sugar, salt, and vanilla. Set over medium heat, stirring occasionally, until the mixture is warm and begins to steam, about 5 minutes. Stir in the melted white chocolate.

In a medium bowl, whisk the egg yolks until smooth. Carefully whisk half of the warm milk mixture into the egg yolks, one ladleful at a time, until the egg mixture is warmed. Whisk the egg-milk mixture back into the saucepan. Cook the mixture over medium heat, stirring constantly with a wooden spoon, until it's thick enough to coat the back of the spoon and registers around 175°F on an instant-read thermometer, about 5 to 7 minutes. Be careful not to boil the mixture.

Immediately strain the mixture through the fine strainer into the prepared ice bath. Stir in the orange zest. Cool the custard in the ice bath until it reaches room temperature, stirring often. Press plastic wrap against the custard and refrigerate until chilled, about 4 hours or up to 1 day.

Pour the chilled mixture into an ice cream maker. Freeze according to the manufacturer's directions. Transfer the ice cream to an airtight container, press plastic wrap against the ice cream, and freeze, at least 2 hours.

> *Tip:* Be sure to use high-quality white chocolate, which should contain cocoa butter as one of the first ingredients on the label.

## SALTED MACADAMIA NUT COOKIES

**MAKES ABOUT 16 COOKIES**

$1\frac{1}{2}$ **cups all-purpose flour**

**1 teaspoon baking soda**

$\frac{1}{4}$ **teaspoon baking powder**

$\frac{1}{4}$ **teaspoon fine sea salt,
  plus more for sprinkling**

**4 ounces (1 stick) unsalted butter,
  at room temperature**

$\frac{1}{2}$ **cup granulated sugar**

$\frac{1}{2}$ **cup packed light brown sugar**

**1 large egg**

**1 large egg yolk**

**1 tablespoon milk**

**1 teaspoon vanilla extract**

**1 cup macadamia nuts, chopped**

Preheat the oven to 350°F. Line baking sheets with parchment paper or silicone baking mats.

In a medium bowl, whisk together the flour, baking soda, baking powder, and salt.

In a large bowl, use an electric mixer to beat the butter and sugars on medium-high speed until well combined and smooth. Beat in the egg, egg yolk, milk, and vanilla. On low speed, add the flour mixture and beat until combined. Fold in the macadamia nuts with a rubber spatula.

Using a spoon or spring-loaded scoop, drop 2 tablespoon–sized balls of dough onto the prepared baking sheets. Flatten slightly with the palm of your hand. Sprinkle dough lightly and evenly with fine sea salt.

Bake for about 10 to 12 minutes, or until the edges are slightly browned. Let cool on baking sheets for 5 minutes before removing to wire racks to cool completely. Freeze the cookies until firm, at least 1 hour. The cookies can be stored in airtight containers in the freezer for up to 1 month.

**TO ASSEMBLE,** top one cookie with a scoop of ice cream. Place another cookie on top of the ice cream and gently press down to form a sandwich. Immediately place the sandwich in the freezer. Repeat for the remaining cookies. Freeze for at least 1 hour before serving.

# Double Cookies and Cream Ice Cream Sandwich

*Although this ice cream sandwich has double the cookies, there's no need for a glass of milk because it also has double the cream! This sandwich is like a giant frozen version of the Oreo cookies everyone loves, with even more Oreo cookies in the filling. Who could resist?*

## COOKIES AND CREAM ICE CREAM

**MAKES ABOUT 1 QUART**

- 1½ **cups whole milk**
- 1½ **cups heavy cream**
- ½ **cup granulated sugar**
- ¼ **teaspoon fine sea salt**
- ½ **teaspoon vanilla extract**
- 4 **large egg yolks**
- 15 **Oreo cookies, coarsely chopped (about 1½ cups)**

Prepare an ice bath by filling a large bowl with ice cubes and 1 to 2 cups of water. Place a medium bowl fitted with a fine strainer inside the ice bath.

In a medium saucepan, combine the milk, cream, sugar, salt, and vanilla. Set over medium heat, stirring occasionally, until the mixture is warm and begins to steam, about 5 minutes.

In a medium bowl, whisk together the egg yolks until smooth. Carefully whisk half of the warm milk mixture into the egg yolks, one ladleful at a time, until the egg mixture is warmed. Whisk the egg-milk mixture back into the saucepan. Cook the mixture over medium heat, stirring constantly, until it's thick enough to coat the back of the spoon and registers around 175°F, about 5 to 7 minutes. Be careful not to boil the mixture.

Immediately strain the mixture through the fine strainer into the prepared ice bath. Cool the custard in the ice bath until it reaches room temperature, stirring often. Press plastic wrap against the custard and refrigerate until chilled, about 4 hours or up to 1 day.

Pour the chilled mixture into an ice cream maker. Freeze according to the manufacturer's directions. In the last 5 minutes of churning, add the Oreo cookies to the mixture. Transfer the ice cream to an airtight container, press plastic wrap against the ice cream surface, and freeze until it is firm and the flavor is ripened, at least 2 hours.

## COCOA COOKIES

**MAKES ABOUT 18 COOKIES**

**1 cup plus 2 tablespoons all-purpose flour**

**$^1/_4$ cup plus 2 tablespoons unsweetened Dutch-process cocoa powder**

**$^3/_4$ teaspoon baking soda**

**$^1/_2$ teaspoon fine sea salt**

**6 ounces (1$^1/_2$ sticks) unsalted butter, at room temperature**

**$^3/_4$ cup granulated sugar**

**2 large eggs**

**$^1/_2$ teaspoon vanilla extract**

Preheat the oven to 375°F. Line large baking sheets with parchment paper or silicone baking mats.

In a medium bowl, sift together the flour, cocoa powder, baking soda, and salt.

In a large bowl, use an electric mixer to beat the butter and sugar on medium-high speed until smooth and well combined, 1 to 2 minutes. Beat in the eggs and vanilla. On low speed, gradually add the flour mixture and beat until combined.

Using a spoon or spring-loaded scoop, drop 2 tablespoon–sized balls of dough on the prepared baking sheets. Slightly flatten each ball of dough. Bake for 9 to 10 minutes, rotating sheets halfway through. Let cool on baking sheets for 5 minutes before removing the cookies to wire racks to cool completely. Freeze the cookies until firm, at least 1 hour. The cookies can be stored in airtight containers in the freezer for up to 1 month.

**TO ASSEMBLE,** top one cookie with a scoop of ice cream. Place another cookie on top of the ice cream and gently press down to form a sandwich. Immediately place the sandwich in the freezer. Repeat for the remaining cookies. Freeze for at least 1 hour before serving.

*Tip:* Add more cookie madness by rolling the edges of these sandwiches in crushed Oreo cookies.

# Oatmeal Raisin Ice Cream Sandwich

## MAKES ABOUT 13 ICE CREAM SANDWICHES

*The warm and hearty flavors of Oatmeal Raisin Cookies and Butter Pecan Ice Cream may not have been your childhood favorite because, let's face it, if it didn't have sprinkles or chocolate, it wasn't really dessert. However, one taste of this buttery and crunchy ice cream with that chewy and cinnamon-scented cookie is sure to convert anyone into an oatmeal raisin fan.*

## BUTTER PECAN ICE CREAM

### MAKES ABOUT 1 QUART

**2 tablespoons unsalted butter**
**1 cup pecans, chopped**
**1/4 teaspoon fine sea salt**
**1 1/2 cups whole milk**
**1 1/2 cups heavy cream**
**1 cup packed light brown sugar, divided**
**1 teaspoon vanilla extract**
**4 large egg yolks**

In a small skillet set over medium heat, melt the butter. Add the pecans and salt and cook, stirring frequently, until the mixture is lightly browned, 5 to 6 minutes. Let cool. Store the buttered pecans in a container at room temperature until ready to use.

Prepare an ice bath by filling a large bowl with ice cubes and 1 to 2 cups of water. Place a medium bowl fitted with a fine strainer inside the ice bath.

In a medium saucepan, combine the milk, cream, 3/4 cup sugar, and vanilla. Set over medium heat, stirring occasionally, until the mixture is warm and begins to steam, about 5 minutes.

In a medium bowl, whisk together the egg yolks and remaining 1/4 cup sugar. Carefully whisk half of the warm milk mixture into the yolks, one ladleful at a time, until the egg mixture is warmed. Whisk the egg-milk mixture back into the saucepan. Cook the mixture over medium heat, stirring constantly, until it's thick enough to coat the back of the spoon, about 5 to 7 minutes. Be careful not to boil the mixture.

Immediately strain the mixture through the fine strainer into the prepared ice bath. Cool the custard in the ice bath until it reaches room temperature, stirring often. Press plastic wrap against the custard and refrigerate until chilled, about 4 hours or up to 1 day.

Pour the chilled mixture into an ice cream maker. Freeze according to the manufacturer's directions. In the last 5 minutes of freezing, add the buttered pecans to the ice cream mixture. Transfer the ice cream to an airtight container, press plastic wrap against the ice cream, and freeze until it is firm, at least 2 hours.

# OATMEAL RAISIN COOKIES

**MAKES ABOUT 26 COOKIES**

1$\frac{1}{2}$ **cups all-purpose flour**
$\frac{1}{2}$ **teaspoon fine sea salt**
$\frac{1}{2}$ **teaspoon baking powder**
**1 teaspoon baking soda**
$\frac{1}{2}$ **teaspoon ground cinnamon**
**8 ounces (2 sticks) unsalted butter, at room temperature**
**1 cup granulated sugar**
**1 cup packed light brown sugar**
**2 large eggs**
**1 teaspoon vanilla extract**
**3 cups old-fashioned rolled oats**
**1 cup raisins**

Preheat the oven to 350°F. Line large baking sheets with parchment paper or silicone baking mats.

In a medium bowl, whisk together the flour, salt, baking powder, baking soda, and cinnamon.

In a large bowl, use an electric mixer to beat the butter and sugars on medium-high speed until smooth and well combined, about 1 to 2 minutes. Beat in the eggs and vanilla. On low speed, gradually add the flour mixture and beat until just combined. Use a rubber spatula to stir in the oats and raisins.

Using a spoon or spring-loaded scoop, drop 2 tablespoon–sized balls of dough onto prepared baking sheets.

Bake for about 12 to 15 minutes, or until the edges are slightly browned, rotating the baking sheets halfway through. Let the cookies cool on baking sheets for 5 minutes before removing to wire racks to cool completely. Freeze the cookies until firm, at least 1 hour. The cookies can be stored in airtight containers in the freezer for up to 1 month.

**TO ASSEMBLE,** top one cookie with a scoop of ice cream. Place another cookie on top of the ice cream and gently press down to form a sandwich. Immediately place the sandwich in the freezer. Repeat for the remaining cookies. Freeze for at least 1 hour before serving.

# Chocolate

**T**HERE'S A REASON CHOCOLATE IS SO POPULAR—ALMOST EVERYONE loves the stuff. In my opinion, chocolate is among the greatest pleasures of life. Whether you're celebrating a success or nursing a broken heart, chocolate is bound to make you feel happy inside. In fact, scientific findings have suggested that some of the chemicals in chocolate trigger pleasurable sensations in our brains. As if you needed more reasons to eat chocolate!

I refuse to believe anything without chocolate is actually a dessert. That is why I had to dedicate an entire chapter in this book to chocolate. Sure, chocolate is great on its own, but when paired with the right ingredients, it is nothing short of magical. So go ahead: Flip through the next few pages, and just try to stop your mouth from watering!

# Grasshopper Ice Cream Sandwich

*In this cool confection, chewy and thick Chocolate Sugar Cookies stand up to the refreshing zing of homemade Mint Chocolate Chip Ice Cream. A chocolate lover's dream sandwich, this is the perfect frosty treat for a sultry summer afternoon.*

## MINT CHOCOLATE CHIP ICE CREAM

### MAKES ABOUT 1 QUART

$1^1/_2$ **cups whole milk**
$1^1/_2$ **cups heavy cream**
$^3/_4$ **cup granulated sugar, divided**
$^1/_4$ **teaspoon fine sea salt**
**4 large egg yolks**
$^1/_2$ **teaspoon vanilla extract**
**1 teaspoon peppermint extract**
**4 to 5 drops green food coloring (optional)**
**1 cup semisweet mini chocolate chips**

Prepare an ice bath by filling a large bowl with ice cubes and 1 to 2 cups of water. Place a medium bowl fitted with a fine strainer inside the ice bath.

In a medium saucepan, combine the milk, cream, $^1/_2$ cup sugar, and salt. Set over medium heat, stirring occasionally, until the mixture is warm and begins to steam, about 5 minutes.

In a medium bowl, whisk together the egg yolks and the remaining $^1/_4$ cup sugar. Carefully whisk half of the warm milk mixture into the egg yolks, one ladleful at a time, until the egg mixture is warmed. Whisk the egg-milk mixture back into the saucepan. Cook the mixture over medium heat, stirring constantly with a wooden spoon, until the mixture is thick enough to coat the back of the spoon and registers around 175°F on an instant-read thermometer, about 5 to 7 minutes. Be careful not to boil the mixture.

Immediately strain the mixture through the fine strainer into the prepared ice bath. Stir in the extracts and food coloring, if using. Cool the custard in the ice bath until it reaches room temperature, stirring often. Press plastic wrap against the surface of the custard and refrigerate until chilled, about 4 hours or up to 1 day.

Pour the chilled custard into an ice cream maker and freeze according to the manufacturer's directions. Add the chocolate chips during the last 5 minutes of churning. Transfer the ice cream to an airtight container, press plastic wrap against the ice cream surface, and freeze until the ice cream is firm and the flavor is ripened, at least 2 hours.

> *Tip:* Instead of miniature chocolate chips, try adding chopped chocolate peppermint patties or Andes mints.

## CHOCOLATE SUGAR COOKIES

**MAKES ABOUT 18 COOKIES**

1 $^3/_4$ **cups plus 2 tablespoons all-purpose flour**

$^1/_2$ **cup unsweetened Dutch-process cocoa powder**

$^3/_4$ **teaspoon baking soda**

$^1/_2$ **teaspoon baking powder**

$^1/_2$ **teaspoon fine sea salt**

6 **ounces (1**$^1/_2$ **sticks) unsalted butter, at room temperature**

1 $^1/_2$ **cups granulated sugar, divided**

2 **large eggs**

1 $^1/_2$ **teaspoons vanilla extract**

Preheat the oven to 350°F. Line large baking sheets with parchment paper or silicone baking mats.

In a medium bowl, sift together the flour, cocoa powder, baking soda, baking powder, and salt.

In a large bowl, use an electric mixer to beat the butter and 1 cup sugar on medium-high speed until well combined and smooth. Beat in the eggs and vanilla. On low speed, add the flour mixture and beat until combined.

Place the remaining $^1/_2$ cup sugar in a shallow dish. Roll the dough into 2 tablespoon–sized balls, then roll in the sugar. Place on prepared baking sheets and flatten with the bottom of a measuring cup to a 2-inch diameter.

Bake for about 10 to 12 minutes, or until the cookies are set. Let cool on baking sheets for 5 minutes before removing to wire racks to cool completely. Freeze the cookies until firm, at least 1 hour. The cookies can be stored in airtight containers in the freezer for up to 1 month.

**TO ASSEMBLE,** top one cookie with a scoop of ice cream. Place another cookie on top of the ice cream and gently press down to form a sandwich. Immediately place the sandwich in the freezer. Repeat for the remaining cookies. Freeze for at least 1 hour before serving.

# Chocolate Malt Ice Cream Sandwich

*Travel back in time to those adorable old-fashioned diners where kids and canoodling couples gulped down thick and frosty malted milkshakes with bright red straws. Malted milk, with its hearty and slightly grainy flavor, works wonders with chocolate in this retro-inspired sandwich.*

## MALTED VANILLA ICE CREAM

**MAKES ABOUT 1 QUART**

**1½ cups whole milk**
**1½ cups heavy cream**
**¾ cup granulated sugar, divided**
**½ cup plain malted milk powder**
**¼ teaspoon fine sea salt**
**1 teaspoon vanilla extract**
**4 large egg yolks**

Prepare an ice bath by filling a large bowl with ice cubes and 1 to 2 cups of water. Place a medium bowl fitted with a fine strainer inside the ice bath.

In a medium saucepan, combine the milk, cream, ½ cup sugar, milk powder, salt, and vanilla. Set over medium heat, stirring occasionally, until the mixture is warm and begins to steam, about 5 minutes.

In a medium bowl, whisk together the egg yolks and the remaining ¼ cup sugar. Carefully whisk half of the warm milk mixture into the egg yolks, one ladleful at a time, until the egg mixture is warmed. Whisk the egg-milk mixture back into the saucepan. Cook the mixture over medium heat, stirring constantly with a wooden spoon, until the mixture is thick enough to coat the back of the spoon and registers around 175°F on an instant-read thermometer, about 5 to 7 minutes. Be careful not to boil the mixture.

Immediately strain the mixture through the fine strainer into the prepared ice bath. Cool the custard in the ice bath until it reaches room temperature, stirring often. Press plastic wrap against the surface of the custard and refrigerate until chilled, about 4 hours or up to 1 day.

Pour the chilled mixture into an ice cream maker and freeze according to the manufacturer's directions. Transfer the ice cream to an airtight container, press plastic wrap against the surface of the ice cream, and freeze until firm and the flavor is ripened, at least 2 hours.

# CHOCOLATE MALT COOKIES

## MAKES ABOUT 20 COOKIES

1 3/4 cups all-purpose flour

1/2 cup unsweetened Dutch-process cocoa powder

1/3 cup plain malted milk powder

1 teaspoon baking soda

1/2 teaspoon fine sea salt

6 ounces (1 1/2 sticks) unsalted butter, at room temperature

1/2 cup granulated sugar

1/2 cup packed light brown sugar

1 large egg

1 1/2 teaspoons vanilla extract

2 tablespoons sour cream or plain yogurt

Preheat the oven to 350°F. Line large baking sheets with parchment paper or silicone baking mats.

In a medium bowl, sift together the flour, cocoa powder, milk powder, baking soda, and salt.

In a large bowl, use an electric mixer to beat the butter and sugars on medium-high speed until well combined and smooth. Beat in the egg, vanilla, and sour cream. On low speed, add the flour mixture and beat until combined.

Roll dough into 2 tablespoon–sized balls and place on the prepared baking sheets. Flatten with the palm of your hand.

Bake for about 10 to 12 minutes, or until the cookies are set. Let cool on baking sheets for 5 minutes before removing to wire racks to cool completely. Freeze the cookies until frozen, at least 1 hour. Cookies can be stored in airtight containers in the freezer for up to 1 month.

## For Decorating:

**Crushed malted milk ball candies (about 1 cup), for rolling**

TO ASSEMBLE, place the crushed malted milk ball candies in a shallow dish.
Top one cookie with a scoop of ice cream. Place another cookie on top of the ice cream and gently press down to form a sandwich. Roll the edges in the crushed malted milk ball candies and repeat for the remaining cookies. Freeze for at least 1 hour before serving.

Tip: Find plain malted milk powder in most grocery stores next to the other powdered milks or instant drink powders.

# Black Forest Ice Cream Sandwich

*Whoopie pies—those traditional New England treats—are like little cakes in the shape of cookies, and they typically sandwich a thick layer of frosting. In this recipe, Chocolate Whoopie Pies sandwich fresh Cherry Ice Cream to make a frozen version of black forest cake. You don't have to be from New England to enjoy these sandwiches!*

## CHERRY ICE CREAM

**MAKES ABOUT 1 QUART**

1$\frac{1}{2}$ **cups whole milk**
1$\frac{1}{2}$ **cups heavy cream**
$\frac{3}{4}$ **cup granulated sugar, divided**
$\frac{1}{4}$ **teaspoon fine sea salt**
**5 large egg yolks**
1$\frac{1}{2}$ **cups fresh pitted sweet dark cherries**
**1 teaspoon vanilla extract**

Prepare an ice bath by filling a large bowl with ice cubes and 1 to 2 cups of water. Place a medium bowl fitted with a fine strainer inside the ice bath.

In a medium saucepan, combine the milk, cream, $\frac{1}{2}$ cup sugar, and salt. Set over medium heat, stirring occasionally, until the mixture is warm and begins to steam, about 5 minutes.

In a medium bowl, whisk together the egg yolks and the remaining $\frac{1}{4}$ cup sugar. Carefully whisk half of the warm milk mixture into the egg yolks, one ladleful at a time, until the egg mixture is warmed. Whisk the egg-milk mixture back into the saucepan. Cook the mixture over medium heat, stirring constantly, until the mixture is thick enough to coat the back of the spoon and registers around 175°F, about 5 to 7 minutes. Be careful not to boil the mixture.

Immediately remove from the heat and stir in the cherries. Let the mixture sit for 10 to 15 minutes, or until slightly cooled.

With an immersion blender, food processor, or blender, carefully puree the mixture until smooth. Add in the vanilla. Strain the mixture through the fine strainer into the prepared ice bath. Cool the custard in the ice bath until it reaches room temperature, stirring often.

Press plastic wrap against the surface of the custard and refrigerate until chilled, about 4 hours or up to 1 day.

Pour the chilled mixture into an ice cream maker. Freeze according to the manufacturer's directions. Transfer the ice cream to an airtight container, press plastic wrap against the ice cream, and freeze until it is firm, at least 2 hours.

## CHOCOLATE WHOOPIE PIES

**MAKES ABOUT 28
WHOOPIE PIE HALVES**

**1³/₄ cups all-purpose flour**

**²/₃ cup unsweetened cocoa powder**

**1¹/₂ teaspoons baking soda**

**¹/₂ teaspoon fine sea salt**

**4 ounces (1 stick) unsalted butter,
  at room temperature**

**¹/₂ cup granulated sugar**

**¹/₂ cup packed light brown sugar**

**1 large egg**

**1 teaspoon vanilla extract**

**1¹/₄ cups whole milk**

Preheat the oven to 375°F. Line large baking sheets with parchment paper or silicone baking mats.

In a medium bowl, sift together the flour, cocoa powder, baking soda, and salt.

In a large bowl, use an electric mixer to beat the butter and sugars on medium-high speed until light and fluffy, about 3 minutes. Add the egg and beat for an additional 2 minutes. Add in the vanilla. On low speed, gradually add half of the flour mixture. Gradually add the milk and beat until combined. Add the remaining flour mixture and beat until combined.

Drop 2 tablespoon–sized balls of dough about 2¹/₂ inches apart on prepared baking sheets.

Bake for about 10 minutes, or until the whoopie pie halves are set and spring back when gently pressed. Do not over-bake. Let the whoopie pie halves cool on pans for 5 minutes, then remove to wire racks to cool completely. Freeze the whoopie pie halves until frozen, at least 1 hour. Whoopie pie halves can be stored in airtight containers in the freezer for up to 1 month.

**TO ASSEMBLE,** top one whoopie pie half with a scoop of ice cream. Place another whoopie pie half on top of the ice cream and gently press down to form a whoopie pie sandwich. Repeat for the remaining whoopie pies. Freeze for at least 1 hour before serving.

# Chocolate Hazelnut Ice Cream Sandwich

*To me, life would not be complete without chocolate hazelnut spread. This sandwich combines Chocolate Hazelnut Ice Cream and Chocolate Hazelnut Cookies with the extra bonus of crunchy chopped hazelnuts around the edges. It's absolute perfection.*

## CHOCOLATE HAZELNUT ICE CREAM

### MAKES ABOUT 1 QUART

1½ **cups whole milk**

1½ **cups heavy cream**

½ **teaspoon vanilla extract**

½ **cup granulated sugar**

¼ **teaspoon fine sea salt**

4 **large egg yolks**

1 **cup chocolate hazelnut spread (such as Nutella)**

Prepare an ice bath by filling a large bowl with ice cubes and 1 to 2 cups of water. Place a medium bowl fitted with a fine strainer inside the ice bath.

In a medium saucepan, combine the milk, cream, vanilla, sugar, and salt. Set over medium heat, stirring occasionally, until the mixture is warm and begins to steam, about 5 minutes.

In a medium bowl, whisk together the egg yolks until smooth. Carefully whisk half of the warm milk mixture into the egg yolks, one ladleful at a time, until the egg mixture is warmed. Whisk the egg-milk mixture back into the saucepan. Cook the mixture over medium heat, stirring constantly with a wooden spoon, until the mixture is thick enough to coat the back of the spoon and registers around 175°F on an instant-read thermometer, about 5 to 7 minutes. Be careful not to boil the mixture.

Immediately strain the mixture through the fine strainer into the prepared ice bath. Stir in the chocolate hazelnut spread and mix for several minutes until dissolved. Don't worry if the chocolate hazelnut spread does not dissolve completely. Cool the custard in the ice bath until it reaches room temperature, stirring often. Press plastic wrap against the surface of the custard and refrigerate until chilled, about 4 hours or up to 1 day.

Pour the chilled mixture into an ice cream maker. Freeze according to the manufacturer's directions. Transfer the ice cream to an airtight container, press plastic wrap against the surface of the ice cream, and freeze until it is firm and the flavor is ripened, at least 2 hours.

## CHOCOLATE HAZELNUT COOKIES

**MAKES ABOUT 18 COOKIES**

1¼ **cups all-purpose flour**

½ **cup unsweetened cocoa powder**

1 **teaspoon baking soda**

½ **teaspoon fine sea salt**

4 **ounces (1 stick) unsalted butter, at room temperature**

½ **cup granulated sugar**

½ **cup packed light brown sugar**

½ **cup chocolate hazelnut spread (such as Nutella)**

1 **large egg**

1 **teaspoon vanilla**

2 **tablespoons milk**

Preheat the oven to 350°F. Line large baking sheets with parchment paper or silicone baking mats.

In a medium bowl, sift together the flour, cocoa powder, baking soda, and salt.

In a large bowl, beat the butter and sugars on medium-high speed until smooth and well combined. Add the chocolate hazelnut spread and beat until combined. Add the egg, vanilla, and milk, and beat until combined. On low speed, gradually add the flour mixture and beat until combined. Cover the dough with plastic wrap and chill in the refrigerator for at least 15 minutes or up to 2 days.

Drop 2 tablespoon–sized balls of dough onto prepared baking sheets. Bake for 10 to 12 minutes, or until the cookies are set. Remove the pans to wire racks to cool completely. Freeze the cookies until frozen, at least 1 hour. Cookies can be stored in airtight containers in the freezer for up to 1 month.

### For decorating:

**Chopped hazelnuts (about 1 cup), for rolling**

**TO ASSEMBLE,** top one cookie with a scoop of ice cream. Place another cookie on top of the ice cream and gently press down to form a sandwich. Roll the edges in the chopped hazelnuts and repeat for the remaining cookies. Freeze for at least 1 hour before serving.

# Chocolate Coconut Ice Cream Sandwich

*A giant frozen version of those famous Mounds candy bars, this ice cream sandwich packs big flavor in each bite. It includes two different types of coconut: cream of coconut and coconut flakes; and two different types of chocolate: cocoa powder and semisweet chocolate. If you enjoy this classic flavor combination, you'll love these beautiful sandwiches.*

## COCONUT ICE CREAM

### MAKES ABOUT 1 QUART

- 1¼ cups whole milk
- 1¼ cups heavy cream
- 1 (15-ounce) can cream of coconut
- ⅓ cup granulated sugar
- ¼ teaspoon fine sea salt
- ½ teaspoon vanilla extract
- 4 large egg yolks

Prepare an ice bath by filling a large bowl with ice cubes and 1 to 2 cups of water. Place a medium bowl fitted with a fine strainer inside the ice bath.

In a medium saucepan, combine the milk, cream, cream of coconut, sugar, salt, and vanilla. Set over medium heat, stirring occasionally, until the mixture is warm and begins to steam, about 5 minutes.

In a medium bowl, whisk the egg yolks until light in color. Carefully whisk half of the warm milk mixture into the egg yolks, one ladleful at a time, until the egg mixture is warmed. Whisk the egg-milk mixture back into the saucepan. Cook the mixture over medium heat, stirring constantly with a wooden spoon, until the mixture is thick enough to coat the back of the spoon and registers around 175°F on an instant-read thermometer, about 5 to 7 minutes. Be careful not to boil the mixture.

Immediately strain the mixture through the fine strainer into the prepared ice bath. Cool the custard in the ice bath until it reaches room temperature, stirring often. Press plastic wrap against the surface of the custard and refrigerate until chilled, about 4 hours or up to 1 day.

Pour the chilled custard into an ice cream maker and freeze according to the manufacturer's directions. Transfer the ice cream to an airtight container, press plastic wrap against the ice cream surface, and freeze until it is firm and the flavor is ripened, at least 4 hours.

# DOUBLE CHOCOLATE COOKIES

## MAKES ABOUT 20 COOKIES

**1 cup all-purpose flour**

**$^1/_3$ cup unsweetened Dutch-process cocoa powder**

**1 teaspoon baking powder**

**$^1/_4$ teaspoon fine sea salt**

**4 ounces (1 stick) unsalted butter, at room temperature**

**$^1/_4$ cup granulated sugar**

**$^3/_4$ cup packed light brown sugar**

**1 large egg**

**1 large egg yolk**

**$^1/_2$ teaspoon vanilla extract**

**8 ounces semisweet chocolate, chopped**

Preheat the oven to 350°F. Line baking sheets with parchment paper or silicone baking mats.

In a medium bowl, sift together the flour, cocoa powder, baking powder, and salt.

In a large bowl, use an electric mixer to beat the butter and sugars on medium-high speed until well combined and smooth. Add the egg and egg yolk and beat until combined. Add the vanilla extract. On low speed, gradually add the flour mixture. Fold in the chopped chocolate with a rubber spatula.

Using a spoon or spring-loaded scoop, drop 2 tablespoon–sized balls of dough onto the prepared baking sheets.

Bake for about 10 minutes, or until the cookies are set. Let cool on baking sheets for 10 minutes before removing the cookies to wire racks to cool completely. Freeze the cookies until frozen, at least 1 hour. Cookies can be stored in airtight containers in the freezer for up to 1 month.

## *For Decorating:*

**Sweetened shredded coconut (about $^1/_2$ cup), for rolling**

**TO ASSEMBLE,** place the shredded coconut in a shallow dish. Top one cookie with a scoop of ice cream. Place another cookie on top of the ice cream and gently press down to form a sandwich. Roll the edges in the coconut flakes and repeat for the remaining cookies. For best results, freeze the sandwiches overnight. Let stand at room temperature for 5 to 10 minutes before serving.

# Chocolate Orange Ice Cream Sandwich

*I adore the bright, sweet, and distinct flavor combination of chocolate and orange, which this sandwich happens to showcase delightfully. I dare anyone to say that they don't like this flavor combination after eating one of these sandwiches.*

## ORANGE ICE CREAM

**MAKES ABOUT 1 QUART**

**1¹/₂ cups whole milk**
**1¹/₂ cups heavy cream**
**³/₄ cup sugar, divided**
**¹/₄ teaspoon fine sea salt**
**1 teaspoon vanilla extract**
**5 large egg yolks**
**Juice and zest from 1 large orange**

Prepare an ice bath by filling a large bowl with ice cubes and 1 to 2 cups of water. Place a medium bowl fitted with a fine strainer inside the ice bath.

In a medium saucepan, combine the milk, cream, ¹/₂ cup sugar, salt, and vanilla. Set over medium heat, stirring occasionally, until the mixture is warm and begins to steam, about 5 minutes.

In a medium bowl, whisk together the egg yolks and remaining ¹/₄ cup sugar. Carefully whisk half of the warm milk mixture into the egg yolks, one ladleful at a time, until the egg mixture is warmed. Whisk the egg-milk mixture back into the saucepan. Cook the mixture over medium heat, stirring constantly with a wooden spoon, until the mixture is thick enough to coat the back of the spoon and registers around 175°F on an instant-read thermometer, about 5 to 7 minutes. Be careful not to boil the mixture.

Stir in the orange juice, then immediately strain the mixture through the fine strainer into the prepared ice bath. Stir in the orange zest. Cool the custard in the ice bath until it reaches room temperature, stirring often. Press plastic wrap against the surface of the custard and refrigerate until chilled, about 4 hours or up to 1 day.

Pour the chilled custard into an ice cream

maker and freeze according to the manufacturer's directions. Transfer the ice cream to an airtight container, press plastic wrap against the ice cream surface, and freeze until it is firm and the flavor is ripened, at least 2 hours.

## FUDGE BROWNIES

**MAKES ABOUT 32 BROWNIES**

1¼ **cups all-purpose flour**
½ **teaspoon fine sea salt**
¾ **teaspoon baking powder**
6 **ounces unsweetened chocolate, chopped**
7 **ounces (1¾ sticks) unsalted butter**
2 **cups granulated sugar**
4 **large eggs**
2 **teaspoons vanilla extract**

Preheat the oven to 325°F. Spray two 8 x 8-inch baking pans with nonstick cooking spray. Line baking pans with parchment paper or foil, leaving an overhang, and spray with nonstick cooking spray.

In a medium bowl, whisk together the flour, salt, and baking powder.

Place the chocolate and butter in a large microwave-safe bowl. Microwave the mixture in 20-second bursts, stirring between each burst, until the chocolate is melted and the mixture is smooth. Gradually whisk in the sugar.

Add the eggs, one at a time, whisking after each addition, until completely combined. Whisk in the vanilla. Gradually add the flour mixture, folding with a rubber spatula to combine.

Divide the batter evenly between the prepared pans. Bake until a toothpick inserted into the center of the brownies comes out with just a few moist crumbs attached, about 20 minutes. Do not over-bake. Let the brownie sheets cool completely in pans on wire racks. Cover brownie sheets with foil and freeze until firm, about 1 hour or up to 1 week.

TO ASSEMBLE, allow the ice cream to sit at room temperature until softened, about 5 to 10 minutes. Pour about 3 cups of the softened ice cream over one brownie sheet in its pan (you will have leftover ice cream). Using the parchment paper or foil, remove the remaining brownie sheet from its pan. Carefully and gently place the brownie sheet on top of the ice cream layer. Cover with plastic wrap and freeze until firm, at least 4 hours or overnight. Remove the pan from the freezer. Use the parchment to remove the brownies from the pan and cut into 16 square sandwiches. Serve immediately or wrap each sandwich in plastic and return to the freezer for up to 1 week. If serving from the freezer, allow the sandwiches to sit at room temperature for 5 to 10 minutes before serving.

# Peanut Butter Cup Ice Cream Sandwich

MAKES ABOUT 12 ICE CREAM SANDWICHES

*If I were stranded on a deserted island and had only peanut butter and chocolate to eat, I'd be happy. When two of my favorite flavors come together in this ice cream sandwich, I can't help but close my eyes with every bite as my taste buds savor a small moment of bliss.*

## DOUBLE CHOCOLATE ICE CREAM

**MAKES ABOUT 1 QUART**

1½ **cups whole milk**

1½ **cups heavy cream**

³⁄₄ **cup granulated sugar, divided**

¼ **cup unsweetened cocoa powder, preferably Dutch-process, sifted**

¼ **teaspoon fine sea salt**

½ **teaspoon vanilla extract**

8 **ounces bittersweet or semisweet chocolate (about 2 cups), melted**

4 **large egg yolks**

Prepare an ice bath by filling a large bowl with ice cubes and 1 to 2 cups of water. Place a medium bowl fitted with a fine strainer inside the ice bath.

In a medium saucepan, combine the milk, cream, ½ cup sugar, cocoa powder, salt, and vanilla. Set over medium heat, stirring occasionally, until the mixture is warm and begins to steam. Stir in the melted chocolate.

Whisk together the egg yolks and remaining ¼ cup sugar. Carefully whisk half of the warm milk mixture into the egg yolks, one ladleful at a time, until the egg mixture is warmed. Whisk the egg-milk mixture back into the saucepan. Cook the mixture over medium heat, stirring constantly, until the mixture is thick enough to coat the back of the spoon and registers around 175°F, about 5 to 7 minutes. Be careful not to boil the mixture.

Immediately strain the mixture through the fine strainer into the prepared ice bath. Cool the custard in the ice bath until it reaches room temperature, stirring often. Press plastic wrap against the custard and refrigerate until chilled, about 4 hours or up to 1 day.

Pour the mixture into an ice cream maker and freeze according to the manufacturer's directions. Transfer to an airtight container, press plastic wrap against the ice cream, and freeze until it is firm, at least 2 hours.

# PEANUT BUTTER COOKIES

**MAKES ABOUT 24 COOKIES**

1 1/2 **cups all-purpose flour**
1 **teaspoon baking soda**
1/4 **teaspoon baking powder**
1/4 **teaspoon fine sea salt**
6 **ounces (1** 1/2 **sticks) unsalted butter, at room temperature**
1/2 **cup granulated sugar**
1/2 **cup packed light brown sugar**
3/4 **cup creamy peanut butter**
1 **large egg**
1/2 **teaspoon vanilla extract**

Preheat the oven to 350°F. Line large baking sheets with parchment paper or silicone baking mats.

In a medium bowl, whisk together the flour, baking soda, baking powder, and salt.

In a large bowl, beat the butter and sugars on medium-high speed until smooth, 1 to 2 minutes. Beat in the peanut butter until fully combined. Beat in the egg and then the vanilla. On low speed, gradually add the flour mixture, beating until combined.

Drop 2 tablespoon–sized balls of dough on prepared baking sheets, spacing about 2 inches apart. Slightly flatten the dough with the bottom of a measuring cup and press the back of a fork into each ball of dough twice to create a crisscross pattern. Bake for 10 to 12 minutes, rotating halfway through, until the edges are slightly browned. Let cool completely. Freeze the cookies until frozen, at least 1 hour. Cookies can be stored in airtight containers in the freezer for up to 1 month.

## For Decorating:

**Chopped salted peanuts (about 1 cup), for rolling**

**TO ASSEMBLE,** top one cookie with a scoop of ice cream. Place another cookie on top and gently press down to form a sandwich. Roll the edges in the peanuts and repeat for the remaining cookies. Freeze for at least 1 hour before serving.

# Real Dessert

**T**HE RECIPES IN THIS CHAPTER ARE EXTRA SPECIAL BECAUSE VARIOUS "real" desserts that we all know and love inspired them. Whatever you order for dessert at your favorite restaurant or bakery, whatever your family recipes are, I hope there's a treat in here that you will discover is even better in frozen sandwich form.

From Strawberry Cheesecake to Root Beer Float, and from Boston Cream Pie to S'mores, the ice cream sandwiches in this chapter are as fun as they are delectable. Transforming classic desserts into ice cream sandwiches was a blast. I hope you enjoy making and eating these ice cream sandwiches as much as I have.

# Strawberry Cheesecake Ice Cream Sandwich

*This ice cream sandwich is a big hit in my house. It's rich yet fresh, sweet yet tangy, and smooth yet chewy. It tastes almost exactly like a slice of strawberry cheesecake—maybe even better.*

## STRAWBERRY CREAM CHEESE ICE CREAM

### MAKES ABOUT 1 QUART

**1 quart fresh or thawed frozen strawberries, hulled and chopped**

**6 ounces cream cheese, at room temperature**

**$1/2$ cup sour cream**

**$1/2$ cup whole milk**

**$1/3$ cup heavy cream**

**2 teaspoons fresh lemon juice**

**$3/4$ cup granulated sugar**

**$1/4$ teaspoon fine sea salt**

**$1 1/2$ teaspoons vanilla extract**

In the bowl of a blender or food processor, puree all the ingredients until smooth, scraping down the sides of the bowl as necessary. Transfer the mixture to a medium bowl and press plastic wrap against the surface. Refrigerate until completely chilled, at least 30 minutes or up to 1 day.

Pour the chilled mixture into an ice cream maker. Freeze according to the manufacturer's directions. Pour the ice cream into an airtight container and press plastic wrap against the surface. Freeze until firm, at least 2 hours or up to 3 days.

## GRAHAM CRACKER COOKIES

### MAKES ABOUT 20 COOKIES

**$2 1/2$ cups all-purpose flour**

**1 teaspoon baking soda**

**$1/2$ teaspoon fine sea salt**

**1 teaspoon ground cinnamon**

**¾ cup packed dark brown sugar**

**4 ounces (1 stick) unsalted butter, cut into cubes and frozen**

**¼ cup honey**

**¼ cup whole milk**

**1 tablespoon vanilla extract**

In the bowl of a food processor, combine the flour, baking soda, salt, cinnamon, and sugar. Pulse one or two times to combine. Add the cubes of butter and pulse until the mixture resembles coarse meal.

In a liquid measuring cup or small bowl, whisk together the honey, milk, and vanilla. Add the mixture to the food processor and pulse until a soft dough begins to form. Shape the dough into a flat disk and wrap in plastic. Refrigerate until firm, at least 2 hours or overnight.

Preheat the oven to 350°F. Line baking sheets with parchment paper or silicone baking mats.

Using a 2-tablespoon scoop, drop balls of dough onto the prepared baking sheets, spacing at least 2 inches apart. Flatten dough balls with the bottom of a measuring cup.

Bake for about 12 minutes, or until the edges are browned. Let the cookies cool on baking sheets for 5 minutes before removing to wire racks to cool completely. Freeze the cookies until frozen, at least 1 hour. Cookies can be stored in airtight containers in the freezer for up to 1 month.

## For decorating:

**Heart-shaped sprinkles (about ½ cup), for rolling (optional)**

**TO ASSEMBLE,** place the sprinkles in a shallow dish, if using. Top one cookie with a scoop of ice cream. Place another cookie on top of the ice cream and gently press down to form a sandwich. Roll the edges in the sprinkles and repeat for the remaining cookies. Freeze for at least 1 hour before serving.

> *Tip:* If you don't have a food processor, you can use a hand-held dough blender to make the dough.

# Boston Cream Pie Ice Cream Sandwich

· · · · · · · · · · ·MAKES ABOUT 14 SMALL ICE CREAM SANDWICHES· · · · · · · · · ·

*Growing up in the Southwest, I spent my childhood never knowing about Boston cream pie. When I discovered that it's two layers of cake sandwiching a layer of pastry cream, all with chocolate on top, I had to try it. This ice cream sandwich is the frozen version. How great is that?*

## PASTRY CREAM ICE CREAM

### MAKES ABOUT 1 QUART

**1¹/₂ cups whole milk**
**2 teaspoons vanilla extract**
**2 tablespoons all-purpose flour**
**1 tablespoon cornstarch**
**²/₃ cup granulated sugar, divided**
**¹/₄ teaspoon fine sea salt**
**3 large egg yolks**
**1¹/₂ cups heavy cream**

Prepare an ice bath by filling a large bowl with ice cubes and 1 to 2 cups of water. Place a medium bowl fitted with a fine strainer inside the ice bath.

In a medium saucepan, combine the milk, vanilla, flour, cornstarch, ¹/₃ cup sugar, and salt. Set over medium heat, stirring occasionally, until the mixture is warm and tiny bubbles form around the edges of the saucepan, about 3 minutes.

In a medium bowl, whisk the remaining ¹/₃ cup sugar with the egg yolks until completely smooth. Carefully whisk half of the warm milk mixture into the egg yolks, one ladleful at a time, until the egg mixture is warmed. Whisk the egg-milk mixture back into the saucepan. Cook the mixture over medium heat, stirring constantly with a wooden spoon, until the mixture is thick enough to coat the back of the spoon and registers around 175°F on an instant-read thermometer, about 5 to 7 minutes. Be careful not to boil the mixture.

Immediately strain the mixture through the fine strainer into the prepared ice bath. Cool the custard in the ice bath until it reaches room temperature, stirring often. Press plastic wrap against the surface of the custard and refrigerate until chilled, about 4 hours or up to 1 day.

Once the mixture is chilled, stir in the heavy cream. Pour the mixture into an ice cream maker. Freeze according to the manufacturer's directions. Transfer the ice cream to an airtight container, press plastic wrap against the ice cream, and freeze until it is firm and the flavor is ripened, at least 4 hours.

# VANILLA WHOOPIE PIES

**MAKES ABOUT 28
WHOOPIE PIE HALVES**

**2¼ cups all-purpose flour**
**1 teaspoon baking powder**
**½ teaspoon fine sea salt**
**4 ounces (1 stick) unsalted butter,
    at room temperature**
**¾ cup granulated sugar**
**¼ cup packed light brown sugar**
**3 large eggs**
**2 teaspoons vanilla extract**
**⅔ cup whole milk**

Preheat the oven to 375°F. Line baking sheets with parchment paper or silicone baking mats.

In a medium bowl, whisk together the flour, baking powder, and salt.

In a large bowl, beat the butter and sugars on medium-high speed until smooth, about 1 to 2 minutes. Add the eggs, one at a time, until

combined. Add the vanilla. On low speed, gradually add half the flour mixture, the milk, and the remaining flour mixture and beat until combined.

Using a spoon or spring-loaded scoop, drop the batter in 2-tablespoon rounds onto prepared baking sheets, spacing 2 inches apart.

Bake for about 8 to 10 minutes, or until the edges are set and the tops spring back when touched. Let cool before removing to wire racks to cool completely. Freeze the whoopie pie halves until frozen, at least 1 hour. Whoopie pie halves can be stored in airtight containers in the freezer for up to 1 month.

## For Decorating:

**Chocolate ganache (about 1 cup),
    for topping (page 49)**

**TO ASSEMBLE,** top one frozen whoopie pie half with a scoop of ice cream. Place another half on top and gently press down to form a sandwich. Pour 1 tablespoon of the ganache over the sandwich. Place the sandwich on a baking sheet or in a flat container. Repeat for the remaining cookies. Place the ice cream sandwiches in the freezer and chill until the ganache has set, about 30 minutes. Serve or wrap sandwiches in plastic wrap and return to the freezer to store for up to 1 week. Let sit at room temperature before serving.

# Carrot Cake Ice Cream Sandwich

*Carrot cake can sometimes fall a bit flat, but it is considerably better as a frozen delight. The carrots are caramelized with butter and sugar, enhanced with cinnamon, and churned into a rich ice cream. When paired with tangy, slightly crisp, and chewy cream cheese cookies, it's an inviting treat.*

## CARROT CAKE ICE CREAM

**MAKES ABOUT 1 QUART**

**4 tablespoons unsalted butter**

**¹⁄₃ cup packed dark brown sugar**

**1¹⁄₂ cups finely grated carrots (from about 3 medium carrots)**

**1¹⁄₂ cups whole milk**

**1¹⁄₂ cups heavy cream**

**Pinch of fine sea salt**

**¹⁄₃ cup granulated sugar**

**4 large egg yolks**

**2 teaspoons vanilla extract**

**¹⁄₂ teaspoon ground cinnamon**

In a small skillet set over medium heat, cook the butter and brown sugar until the butter is melted and the sugar is dissolved. Add the carrots and cook for about 5 minutes, until the mixture is thick and the carrots are soft. Set aside.

Prepare an ice bath by filling a large bowl with ice cubes and 1 to 2 cups of water. Place a medium bowl fitted with a fine strainer inside the ice bath.

In a medium saucepan, combine the milk, cream, salt, and granulated sugar. Set over medium heat, stirring occasionally, until the mixture is warm and begins to steam, about 5 minutes.

In a small bowl, whisk the egg yolks until smooth and pale in color. Carefully whisk half of the warm milk mixture into the egg yolks, one ladleful at a time, until the egg mixture is warmed. Whisk the egg-milk mixture back into the saucepan. Cook the mixture over medium heat, stirring constantly with a wooden spoon, until the mixture is thick enough to coat the back of the spoon and registers around 175°F on an instant-read thermometer, about 5 to 7 minutes. Be careful not to boil the mixture.

Immediately strain the mixture through the fine strainer into the prepared ice bath. Add the vanilla and cinnamon, stirring to combine.

Add the carrot mixture. Cool the custard in the ice bath until it reaches room temperature, stirring often. Press plastic wrap against the custard and refrigerate until chilled, about 4 hours or up to 1 day.

Pour the chilled custard into an ice cream maker. Freeze according to the manufacturer's directions. Transfer the ice cream to an airtight container, press plastic wrap against the ice cream, and freeze until it is firm, at least 2 hours.

## CREAM CHEESE COOKIES

**MAKES ABOUT 26 COOKIES**

1³/₄ **cups all-purpose flour**
¹/₂ **teaspoon baking powder**
¹/₄ **teaspoon fine sea salt**
**4 ounces (1 stick) unsalted butter, at room temperature**
**4 ounces cream cheese, at room temperature**
³/₄ **cup granulated sugar**
**1 large egg**
**1 teaspoon grated lemon zest**
**1 teaspoon vanilla extract**
¹/₄ **teaspoon almond extract**

In a medium bowl, whisk together the flour, baking powder, and salt.

In a large bowl, beat the butter, cream cheese, and sugar until smooth. Beat in the egg, zest, and extracts. On low speed, add the flour mixture and beat until a soft dough forms. Shape the dough into a flat disk, wrap in plastic, and chill in the refrigerator for at least 4 hours.

Preheat the oven to 375°F. Line baking sheets with parchment paper or silicone baking mats.

Cut the dough in half and return half to the refrigerator. Place the dough between two large sheets of parchment paper on a work surface. Roll the dough out into a ¹/₄-inch thickness, using the parchment to prevent sticking. Cut out 2¹/₂-inch rounds with a circle cookie cutter and place on prepared baking sheets. Repeat with remaining dough.

Bake for about 10 minutes, or until the edges are lightly golden. Let cool completely. Freeze the cookies until frozen, at least 1 hour. Cookies can be stored in airtight containers in the freezer for up to 1 month.

### *For decorating:*

**Finely chopped pecans (about 1 cup), for rolling edges**

**TO ASSEMBLE,** top one cookie with a scoop of ice cream. Place another cookie on top and gently press down to form a sandwich. Roll the edges in the pecans and repeat for the remaining cookies. Freeze for at least 1 hour before serving.

# S'mores Ice Cream Sandwich

*Everybody loves s'mores. What's not to love about graham crackers, marshmallows, and chocolate? This ice cream sandwich takes s'mores to a whole new level. Trust me: You haven't had s'mores until you've had a s'mores ice cream sandwich.*

## S'MORES ICE CREAM

**MAKES ABOUT 1½ QUARTS**

1½ **cups whole milk**
1½ **cups heavy cream**
1 **teaspoon vanilla extract**
¼ **teaspoon fine sea salt**
½ **cup unsweetened cocoa powder, sifted**
½ **cup granulated sugar**
¼ **cup packed light brown sugar**
4 **large egg yolks**
3 **ounces milk chocolate**
⅔ **cup marshmallow fluff**
2 **full graham cracker sheets, crushed**

Prepare an ice bath by filling a large bowl with ice cubes and 1 to 2 cups of water. Place a medium bowl fitted with a fine strainer inside the ice bath.

In a medium saucepan, combine the milk, cream, vanilla, salt, cocoa powder, and granulated sugar. Set over medium heat, stirring occasionally, until the mixture is warm and begins to steam, about 5 minutes.

In a medium bowl, whisk together the brown sugar and egg yolks until smooth. Carefully whisk half of the warm milk mixture into the egg yolks, one ladleful at a time, until the egg mixture is warmed. Whisk the egg-milk mixture back into the saucepan. Cook the mixture over medium heat, stirring constantly with a wooden spoon, until the mixture is thick enough to coat the back of the spoon and registers around 175°F on an instant-read thermometer, about 5 to 7 minutes. Be careful not to boil the mixture.

Immediately strain the mixture through the fine strainer into the prepared ice bath. Cool the custard in the ice bath until it reaches room temperature, stirring often. Press plastic wrap against the surface of the custard and refrigerate until chilled, about 4 hours or up to 1 day.

When ready to freeze the custard, place milk chocolate in a small microwave-safe bowl and microwave in 20-second bursts, stirring between bursts, until melted and smooth.

Pour the chilled custard into an ice cream maker. Freeze according to the manufacturer's directions. During the last 5 minutes of freezing, gradually add the marshmallow fluff, 1 spoonful at a time. Once combined, add the crushed graham crackers and melted chocolate until just combined. Transfer the ice cream to an airtight container, press plastic wrap against the ice cream surface, and freeze until it is firm and the flavor is ripened, at least 2 hours.

## S'MORES COOKIES

### MAKES ABOUT 20 COOKIES

³/₄ cup all-purpose flour

1 cup fine graham cracker crumbs (about 15 whole graham cracker sheets)

1 teaspoon baking soda

¹/₂ teaspoon fine sea salt

4 ounces (1 stick) unsalted butter, at room temperature

¹/₂ cup granulated sugar

¹/₂ cup packed light brown sugar

1 large egg

1 tablespoon milk

1 teaspoon vanilla extract

1 cup miniature milk chocolate chips

³/₄ cup miniature marshmallows

1¹/₂-ounce milk chocolate candy bar, roughly chopped

Preheat the oven to 350°F. Line baking sheets with parchment paper or silicone baking mats.

In a medium bowl, whisk together the flour, graham cracker crumbs, baking soda, and salt.

In a large bowl, use an electric mixer to beat the butter and sugars until light and smooth. Beat in the egg, milk, and vanilla. On low speed, gradually add the flour mixture until just combined. Fold in the miniature chocolate chips with a rubber spatula.

Using a spoon or spring-loaded scoop, drop 2 tablespoon–sized balls of dough onto prepared baking sheets. Flatten slightly with the palm of your hand.

Bake for 8 minutes. Remove the baking sheets from the oven and push 3 to 4 marshmallows and a few pieces of chocolate candy bar into each cookie. Return to the oven and bake for an additional 3 to 4 minutes, or until the edges are set and the marshmallows have puffed slightly. Let cool on baking sheets for 5 minutes before removing to wire racks to cool completely. Freeze the cookies until frozen, at least 1 hour. Cookies can be stored in airtight containers in the freezer for up to 1 month.

## For decorating:

**Chocolate sprinkles (about ¹/₂ cup),
for rolling**

**TO ASSEMBLE,** place the chocolate sprinkles in a shallow dish. Top one cookie with a scoop of ice cream. Place another cookie on top of the ice cream and gently press down to form a sandwich. Roll the edges in the sprinkles and repeat for the remaining cookies. Freeze for at least 1 hour before serving.

# Root Beer Float Ice Cream Sandwich

*When I was younger, it seemed like a root beer float party accompanied every occasion for celebration, especially in school. Whether we were celebrating good grades, a fundraiser, or the end of the school year, I have many memories of friends laughing and sipping on a float. Try this fun twist on that classic drink, which pairs intense Root Beer Ice Cream with sweet Vanilla Bean Cookies.*

## ROOT BEER ICE CREAM

### MAKES ABOUT 1 QUART

1½ **cups whole milk**
1½ **cups heavy cream**
¼ **teaspoon fine sea salt**
¾ **cup granulated sugar, divided**
4 **large egg yolks**
1 **teaspoon vanilla extract**
1 **tablespoon root beer concentrate**

Prepare an ice bath by filling a large bowl with ice cubes and 1 to 2 cups of water. Place a medium bowl fitted with a fine strainer inside the ice bath.

In a medium saucepan, combine the milk, cream, salt, and ½ cup sugar. Set over medium heat, stirring occasionally, until the mixture is warm and begins to steam, about 5 minutes.

In a medium bowl, whisk together the egg yolks and the remaining ¼ cup sugar. Carefully whisk half of the warm milk mixture into the egg yolks, one ladleful at a time, until the egg mixture is warmed. Whisk the egg-milk mixture back into the saucepan. Cook the mixture over medium heat, stirring constantly, until the mixture is thick enough to coat the back of the spoon and registers around 175°F, about 5 to 7 minutes. Be careful not to boil the mixture.

Immediately strain the mixture through the fine strainer into the prepared ice bath. Add the vanilla extract and root beer concentrate, stirring to combine. Cool the custard in the ice bath until at room temperature, stirring often. Press plastic wrap against the custard and refrigerate until chilled, about 4 hours or up to 1 day.

Pour the chilled mixture into an ice cream maker. Freeze according to the manufacturer's directions. Transfer the ice cream to an airtight container, press plastic wrap against the surface of the ice cream, and freeze until it is firm and the flavor is ripened, at least 2 hours.

# VANILLA BEAN COOKIES

**MAKES ABOUT 18 COOKIES**

1³/₄ **cups all-purpose flour**
¹/₄ **teaspoon baking powder**
¹/₂ **teaspoon fine sea salt**
5 **ounces (1¹/₄ sticks) unsalted butter, at room temperature**
1 **cup granulated sugar**
2 **large eggs**
1 **tablespoon milk**
1 **vanilla bean (or 2 teaspoons vanilla extract)**

Preheat the oven to 350°F. Line baking sheets with parchment paper or silicone baking mats.

In a medium bowl, whisk together the flour, baking powder, and salt.

In a large bowl, use an electric mixer to beat the butter and sugar until light and smooth. Beat in the eggs and milk. With a small sharp knife, halve the vanilla bean lengthwise. Scrape the vanilla seeds into the butter mixture and beat until combined. On low speed, gradually add the flour mixture.

Using a spoon or spring-loaded scoop, drop 2 tablespoon–sized balls of dough onto prepared baking sheets. Flatten slightly with the palm of your hand.

Bake for about 10 to 12 minutes, or until the cookies are set. Let cool on baking sheets for 5 minutes before removing to wire racks to cool completely. Freeze the cookies until frozen, at least 1 hour. Cookies can be stored in airtight containers in the freezer for up to 1 month.

## For decorating:

**Rainbow sprinkles (about ¹/₂ cup), for rolling (optional)**

**TO ASSEMBLE,** place the rainbow sprinkles in a shallow dish, if using. Top one cookie with a scoop of ice cream. Place another cookie on top of the ice cream and gently press down to form a sandwich. Roll the edges in the sprinkles and repeat for the remaining cookies. Freeze for at least 1 hour before serving.

> *Tip:* Find root beer concentrate with other extracts and flavorings in the baking aisle of your supermarket.

# Chocolate Caramel Macchiato Ice Cream Sandwich

*There's no need to visit the coffee shop when you're craving a caramel macchiato anymore. In this cookie recipe, caramel is melted and mixed into the cookie dough, so every bite has that distinct sweet taste and chewy texture. With the bold chocolate and coffee flavors of Mocha Ice Cream, this sandwich turns into something extraordinary.*

## MOCHA ICE CREAM

**MAKES ABOUT 1 QUART**

- 1$\frac{1}{2}$ **cups whole milk**
- 1$\frac{1}{2}$ **cups heavy cream**
- $\frac{3}{4}$ **cup granulated sugar, divided**
- $\frac{1}{4}$ **teaspoon fine sea salt**
- **3 tablespoons unsweetened cocoa powder, preferably Dutch-process**
- **2 tablespoons instant espresso powder**
- $\frac{1}{2}$ **teaspoon vanilla extract**
- **4 large egg yolks**

Prepare an ice bath by filling a large bowl with ice cubes and 1 to 2 cups of water. Place a medium bowl fitted with a fine strainer inside the ice bath.

In a medium saucepan, combine the milk, cream, $\frac{1}{2}$ cup sugar, salt, cocoa powder, espresso powder, and vanilla. Set over medium heat, stirring occasionally, until the mixture is warm and begins to steam, about 5 minutes.

In a medium bowl, whisk together the egg yolks and remaining $\frac{1}{4}$ cup sugar. Carefully whisk half of the warm milk mixture into the egg yolks, one ladleful at a time, until the egg mixture is warmed. Whisk the egg-milk mixture back into the saucepan. Cook the mixture over medium heat, stirring constantly with a wooden spoon, until the mixture is thick enough to coat the back of the spoon and registers around 175°F on an instant-read thermometer, about 5 to 7 minutes. Be careful not to boil the mixture.

Immediately strain the mixture through the fine strainer into the prepared ice bath. Cool the custard in the ice bath until it reaches room temperature, stirring often. Press plastic wrap against the surface of the custard and refrigerate until chilled, about 4 hours or up to 1 day.

Pour the chilled mixture into an ice cream maker. Freeze according to the manufacturer's directions. Transfer the ice cream to an airtight container, press plastic wrap against the surface of the ice cream, and freeze until firm, at least 2 hours or up to 3 days.

## CARAMEL COOKIES

**MAKES ABOUT 18 COOKIES**

**6 ounces unwrapped caramel candy squares**

**2 tablespoons heavy cream**

**2 cups all-purpose flour**

**1 teaspoon baking soda**

**¼ teaspoon baking powder**

**¼ teaspoon fine sea salt**

**4 ounces (1 stick) unsalted butter, at room temperature**

**¼ cup granulated sugar**

**¼ cup packed light brown sugar**

**1 large egg**

**1 teaspoon vanilla extract**

Preheat the oven to 350°F. Line baking sheets with parchment paper or silicone baking mats.

Place the caramels and heavy cream in a medium microwave-safe bowl. Microwave in 30-second bursts, stirring between each burst, until the caramels are melted and the mixture is smooth.

In a medium bowl, whisk together the flour, baking soda, baking powder, and salt.

In a large bowl, use an electric mixer to beat the butter and sugars on medium speed until well combined and smooth. Beat in the egg and vanilla. Drizzle in the caramel mixture until combined. On low speed, gradually add the flour mixture until combined.

Using a spoon or spring-loaded scoop, drop 2 tablespoon–sized balls of the dough onto prepared baking sheets.

Bake for about 10 minutes, or until the edges are set. Let cool on baking sheets for 10 minutes before removing to wire racks to cool completely. Freeze the cookies until firm, about 1 hour. Cookies can be stored in airtight containers in the freezer for up to 1 month.

**TO ASSEMBLE,** top one cookie with a scoop of ice cream. Place another cookie on top of the ice cream and gently press down to form a sandwich. Freeze for at least 1 hour before serving.

# Cannoli Ice Cream Sandwich

*Although nothing is deep fried or tube shaped in this ice cream sandwich, the results are just as heavenly as the classic Italian-American dessert. Don't skip the chocolate dip—it really takes this ice cream sandwich to the next level!*

## SWEET RICOTTA ICE CREAM

**MAKES ABOUT 1 QUART**

**1 (15-ounce) container high-quality whole-milk ricotta**

**³/₄ cup whole milk**

**³/₄ cup heavy cream**

**1 cup granulated sugar**

**1 teaspoon grated orange zest**

Place all the ingredients in the bowl of a food processor or blender. Pulse until the mixture is completely smooth. Remove the mixture to a bowl and refrigerate until thoroughly chilled.

Pour the chilled mixture into an ice cream maker. Freeze according to the manufacturer's directions. Transfer the ice cream to an airtight container, press plastic wrap against the surface of the ice cream, and freeze until it is firm and the flavor is ripened, at least 4 hours.

## CANNOLI COOKIES

**MAKES ABOUT 24 COOKIES**

**1³/₄ cups all-purpose flour**

**1 teaspoon baking powder**

**¹/₄ teaspoon fine sea salt**

**¹/₄ teaspoon ground cinnamon**

**4 ounces (1 stick) unsalted butter, at room temperature**

**¹/₂ cup granulated sugar**

**¹/₄ cup packed light brown sugar**

**1 large egg**

**1 teaspoon vanilla extract**

In a medium bowl, whisk together the flour, baking powder, salt, and cinnamon.

In a large bowl, use an electric mixer to beat the butter and sugars on medium-high speed until smooth and well combined, about 1 to 2 minutes. Add the egg and vanilla and beat until combined. On low speed, gradually add the flour mixture until combined. Shape the dough into a 6-inch-long log. Wrap in parchment paper and freeze until firm.

Preheat the oven to 350°F. Line baking sheets with parchment paper or silicone baking mats.

Using a small sharp knife, slice ¼-inch rounds of dough from the log. Place rounds on prepared baking sheets.

Bake for about 10 minutes, or until the edges are lightly browned. Let cool on baking sheets for 2 minutes before removing to wire racks to cool completely. Freeze the cookies until frozen, at least 1 hour. Cookies can be stored in airtight containers in the freezer for up to 1 month.

## For decorating:

**Chocolate Dip (about 1 cup), for dipping (page 50)**

**TO ASSEMBLE,** top one cookie with a scoop of ice cream. Place another cookie on top of the ice cream and gently press down to form a sandwich. Place the sandwich on a parchment-lined baking sheet or container that will store the sandwiches and that will fit in your freezer. Repeat process for the remaining cookies. Freeze until the sandwiches are firm, about 2 hours.

Working with one frozen sandwich at a time, dip half of the sandwich into the melted chocolate, allowing excess to drip back into the bowl. Place the sandwich back on the frozen baking sheet. Repeat with remaining sandwiches and chocolate. Place the sheet of ice cream sandwiches in the freezer and chill until the chocolate has set, about 1 hour. Serve or wrap the sandwiches individually in plastic and store in the freezer for up to 4 days.

*Tip:* For even more texture, roll the edge of the ice cream sandwich that hasn't been dipped in chocolate in chopped pistachios.

# Turtle Ice Cream Sandwich

*The appeal of turtle desserts—a combination of chocolate, caramel, and pecans—is as much about flavor as it is about texture. The richness of the chocolate, the sweet thickness of the caramel, and the nutty crunchiness of the pecans work together to create something splendid that anyone would enjoy. The Turtle Crunch sprinkles called for in the recipe are brown and tan sprinkles that can be found at most supermarkets in the baking aisle or at a baking supply store.*

## CARAMEL-CHOCOLATE SWIRL ICE CREAM

**MAKES ABOUT 1½ QUARTS**

1½ **cups whole milk**
1½ **cups heavy cream**
**1 teaspoon vanilla extract**
½ **cup granulated sugar, divided**
**Pinch of fine sea salt**
**5 large egg yolks**
**1 cup Fudge Swirl (page 50)**
**1 cup Salted Caramel Sauce (page 50)**

Prepare an ice bath by filling a large bowl with ice cubes and 1 to 2 cups of water. Place a medium bowl fitted with a fine strainer inside the ice bath.

In a medium saucepan, combine the milk, cream, vanilla, ¼ cup sugar, and salt. Set over medium heat, stirring occasionally, until the mixture is warm and begins to steam, about 5 minutes.

In a medium bowl, whisk together the egg yolks and the remaining ¼ cup sugar. Carefully whisk half of the warm milk mixture into the egg yolks, one ladleful at a time, until the egg mixture is warmed. Whisk the egg-milk mixture back into the saucepan. Cook the mixture over medium heat, stirring constantly with a wooden spoon, until the mixture is thick enough to coat the back of the spoon and registers around 175°F on an instant-read thermometer, about 5 to 7 minutes. Be careful not to boil the mixture.

Immediately strain the mixture through the fine strainer into the prepared ice bath. Cool the custard in the ice bath until it reaches room temperature, stirring often. Press plastic wrap against the surface of the custard and refrigerate until chilled, about 4 hours or up to 1 day.

While the custard is chilling, make the Fudge Swirl (page 50) and Salted Caramel Sauce (page 50). Keep at room temperature and set aside until ready to use. If making beforehand, Fudge Swirl and Salted Caramel Sauce can be stored in the fridge for up to 2 days, but should be brought to room temperature before they are added to the ice cream so that they are easier to pour.

Pour the chilled mixture into an ice cream maker. Freeze according to the manufacturer's directions. During the last few minutes of freezing, swirl in the Fudge Swirl and Salted Caramel Sauce. Transfer the ice cream to an airtight container, press plastic wrap against the ice cream surface, and freeze until it is firm and the flavor is ripened, at least 4 hours.

## CHOCOLATE, CARAMEL, AND PECAN COOKIES

**MAKES ABOUT 20 COOKIES**

1½ **cups all-purpose flour**
½ **teaspoon baking soda**
½ **teaspoon baking powder**
¼ **teaspoon fine sea salt**
4 **ounces (1 stick) unsalted butter, at room temperature**
¼ **cup granulated sugar**
¾ **cup packed light brown sugar**
1 **large egg**
1 **teaspoon vanilla extract**
½ **cup semisweet chocolate chunks**
½ **cup caramel bits (such as Kraft)**
½ **cup pecans, chopped**

In a small bowl, whisk together the flour, baking soda, baking powder, and salt.

In a large bowl, use an electric mixer to beat the butter and sugars until well combined. Beat in the egg and vanilla. Fold in the chocolate chunks, caramel bits, and pecans with a rubber spatula.

Preheat the oven to 350°F. Line baking sheets with parchment paper or silicone baking mats.

Using a spoon or spring-loaded scoop, drop 2 tablespoon–sized balls of dough onto the prepared baking sheets. Flatten slightly with the palm of your hand.

Bake for about 10 to 12 minutes, or until the edges are slightly browned. Let cool on baking sheets for 5 minutes before removing to wire racks to cool completely. Freeze the cookies until frozen, at least 1 hour. Cookies can be stored in airtight containers in the freezer for up to 1 month.

## For Decorating:

**Turtle Crunch sprinkles (about ½ cup), for rolling (such as Wilton)**

**TO ASSEMBLE,** place the Turtle Crunch sprinkles in a shallow dish. Top one cookie with a scoop of ice cream. Place another cookie on top of the ice cream and gently press down to form a sandwich. Roll the edges in the sprinkles. Immediately place the sandwich in the freezer. Repeat for the remaining cookies. Freeze for at least 2 hours before serving.

# Fruity

**T**HIS CHAPTER WILL HELP YOU GET YOUR RECOMMENDED DAILY DOSE OF fruit in a way you never thought possible. Whether you love berries, bananas, mangoes, or peaches, these ice cream sandwiches are bright and refreshing and brimming with fruity flavor. Although I can't claim that sugar, butter, or cream is particularly healthy, there are a couple of recipes in this chapter that you can serve to friends and family members who follow special diets.

The Flourless Peanut Butter Cookies (page 126) are gluten-free, and both the Dairy-Free Banana Ice Cream (page 127) and Vegan Chocolate Chip Cookies (page 127) are vegan. Serve these selections to your gluten-eating, non-vegan friends, and they'll never know the difference.

# Peanut Butter and Jelly Ice Cream Sandwich

*I can't count the number of PB&J sandwiches I've eaten in my life. However, I can tell you that you've never had a PB&J sandwich quite like this one. Luscious and tangy Raspberry Ice Cream works wonders with the intense peanut butter flavor of these flourless cookies. But what really makes this ice cream sandwich a standout is the coating of crushed salty potato chips around the edges.*

## RASPBERRY ICE CREAM

### MAKES ABOUT 1½ QUARTS

**4 cups fresh or thawed frozen raspberries**

**1½ cups whole milk**

**1½ cups heavy cream**

**¾ cup granulated sugar, divided**

**¼ teaspoon fine sea salt**

**½ teaspoon vanilla extract**

**5 large egg yolks**

**1 tablespoon raspberry liqueur (such as Chambord), optional**

In a food processor or blender, puree the raspberries until smooth. Use a fine strainer to strain the mixture into a medium bowl. Discard any seeds or pulp that remain. Refrigerate the puree until ready to use.

Prepare an ice bath by filling a large bowl with ice cubes and 1 to 2 cups of water. Place a medium bowl fitted with a fine strainer inside the ice bath.

In a medium saucepan, combine the milk, cream, ½ cup sugar, salt, and vanilla. Set over medium heat, stirring occasionally, until the mixture is warm and begins to steam, about 5 minutes.

In a medium bowl, whisk together the egg yolks and the remaining ¼ cup sugar. Carefully whisk half of the warm milk mixture into the egg yolks, one ladleful at a time, until the egg mixture is warmed. Whisk the egg-milk mixture back into the saucepan. Cook the mixture over medium heat, stirring constantly with a wooden spoon, until the mixture is thick enough to coat the back of the spoon and registers around 175°F on an instant-read thermometer, about 5 to 7 minutes. Be careful not to boil the mixture.

Strain the mixture through the fine strainer into the prepared ice bath. Stir in the strained raspberry puree. Cool the custard in the ice bath until it reaches room temperature, stirring often. Press plastic wrap against the surface of the custard and refrigerate until chilled, about 4 hours or up to 1 day.

Pour the custard into an ice cream maker. Freeze according to the manufacturer's directions. During the last minute of freezing, add the raspberry liqueur, if using. Transfer to an airtight container, press plastic wrap against the surface of the ice cream, and freeze until it is firm and the flavor is ripened, at least 2 hours.

## FLOURLESS PEANUT BUTTER COOKIES

**MAKES ABOUT 20 COOKIES**

1½ **cups peanut butter, smooth or chunky**
¾ **cup packed light brown sugar**
¾ **cup granulated sugar**
1 **large egg**
¾ **teaspoon baking soda**
¾ **teaspoon vanilla extract**

Preheat the oven to 350°F. Line large baking sheets with parchment paper or silicone baking mats.

In a medium bowl, use a rubber spatula to mix together all the ingredients until thoroughly combined.

Drop 2 tablespoon–sized balls of dough on prepared baking sheets, spacing about 2 inches apart. Flatten the dough with the bottom of a measuring cup. Bake for 10 to 12 minutes, or until the edges are slightly browned. Let cool on baking sheets for 5 minutes before removing the cookies to wire racks to cool completely. Freeze the cookies until frozen, at least 1 hour. Cookies can be stored in airtight containers in the freezer for up to 1 month.

### For decorating:

**Crushed potato chips (about ½ cup),
   for rolling**

**TO ASSEMBLE,** place the potato chips in a shallow dish. Top one cookie with a scoop of ice cream. Place another cookie on top of the ice cream and gently press down to form a sandwich. Roll the edges in the potato chips and repeat for the remaining cookies. Freeze for at least 1 hour before serving.

# Vegan Banana Chocolate Chip Ice Cream Sandwich

*This ice cream sandwich is so good that no one will ever know that it's vegan and that the ice cream has but one ingredient: bananas! In the Vegan Chocolate Chip Cookies, coconut oil is a fabulous replacement for butter. A mixture of ground flax seeds and water replaces the egg in the dough. Vegan chocolate chips complete the cookies.*

## DAIRY-FREE BANANA ICE CREAM

**MAKES ABOUT 1 QUART**

**8 medium ripe bananas**

Peel and chop the bananas into bite-size pieces. Place the bananas in a single layer on a rimmed baking sheet. Freeze for 1 to 2 hours or overnight.

Place the banana pieces in the bowl of a food processor or blender. If the bananas were frozen overnight, let them sit at room temperature for 10 minutes before pureeing. You may need to do several batches if your processor or blender isn't big enough. Puree the bananas until completely smooth with a soft-serve ice cream consistency, scraping down the sides of the bowl as necessary.

Remove the mixture to an airtight container. Press plastic wrap against the surface of the ice cream and freeze until firmed, about 2 hours or up to several days.

## VEGAN CHOCOLATE CHIP COOKIES

**MAKES ABOUT 20 COOKIES**

**1$\frac{1}{2}$ cups all-purpose flour**
**$\frac{1}{2}$ teaspoon baking soda**
**$\frac{1}{2}$ teaspoon baking powder**
**$\frac{1}{2}$ teaspoon fine sea salt**
**$\frac{1}{2}$ cup coconut oil**
**$\frac{1}{2}$ cup granulated sugar**
**$\frac{1}{2}$ cup packed light brown sugar**
**1 tablespoon ground flaxseed**
**2 tablespoons water**

**1 tablespoon non-dairy milk
(such as almond milk or soy milk)**
**2 teaspoons vanilla extract**
**1 cup vegan (dairy-free) chocolate chips**

Preheat the oven to 375°F. Line large baking sheets with parchment paper or silicone baking mats.

In a small bowl, whisk together the flour, baking soda, baking powder, and salt.

In a large bowl, use an electric mixer to beat the coconut oil and sugars on medium-high speed until well combined and smooth. In a small bowl, combine the flaxseed and water, then add into the mixture. Beat in the non-dairy milk and vanilla. On low speed, gradually add the flour mixture until combined. Fold in the chocolate chips with a rubber spatula.

Using a spoon or spring-loaded scoop, drop 2 tablespoon–sized balls of dough onto prepared baking sheets. Flatten slightly with the palm of your hand.

Bake for about 8 to 10 minutes, or until the edges are slightly browned. Let cool on baking sheets for 5 minutes before removing to wire racks to cool completely. Freeze cookies until frozen, at least 1 hour. Cookies can be stored in airtight containers in the freezer for up to 1 month.

**TO ASSEMBLE,** top one cookie with a scoop of ice cream. Place another cookie on top of the ice cream and gently press down to form a sandwich. Repeat for remaining cookies. Freeze for at least 1 hour before serving.

*Tip:* Find vegan chocolate chips, which are free of dairy, at many supermarkets or specialty health-food stores.

# Pomegranate Ice Cream Sandwich

*A more sophisticated ice cream sandwich, this tasty treat is full of complex and exotic flavors. Fresh, tart, tangy, sweet, slightly pungent, and citrusy, this dessert will take your taste buds on a frozen culinary adventure. Enjoy the ride!*

## POMEGRANATE FROZEN YOGURT

### MAKES ABOUT 1 QUART

**2 cups pomegranate juice**
**1 tablespoon fresh lemon juice**
**1/2 cup granulated sugar, divided**
**2 1/2 cups plain low-fat yogurt**
**1/2 cup whole milk**
**1/4 teaspoon fine sea salt**

Place the pomegranate juice, lemon juice, and 1/4 cup sugar in a small saucepan set over medium heat. Cook, stirring occasionally, until the sugar is dissolved. Reduce heat to medium-low and simmer until the mixture is thick and syruplike, about 45 minutes. Remove from the heat and allow the mixture to cool for at least 30 minutes. Pomegranate syrup can be made ahead of time and stored in a glass airtight container in the refrigerator for up to 6 months.

In a medium bowl, stir together the cooled pomegranate syrup, the remaining 1/4 cup sugar, yogurt, milk, and salt until well combined. If using room-temperature pomegranate syrup, chill the mixture in the refrigerator for 30 minutes.

Pour the mixture into an ice cream maker and freeze according to the manufacturer's directions. Remove the frozen yogurt to an airtight container and press plastic wrap against the surface. Freeze for at least 2 hours or up to 2 days.

## ORANGE CARDAMOM COOKIES

### MAKES ABOUT 18 COOKIES

**1 3/4 cups all-purpose flour**
**1/2 teaspoon baking powder**
**1/4 teaspoon baking soda**
**1 teaspoon ground cardamom**

**¼ teaspoon fine sea salt**

**4 ounces (1 stick) unsalted butter,
  at room temperature**

**2 ounces cream cheese,
  at room temperature**

**¾ cup granulated sugar**

**Zest from 2 small oranges**

**1 large egg**

Preheat the oven to 350° F. Line large baking sheets with parchment paper or silicone baking mats.

In a medium bowl, whisk the flour, baking powder, baking soda, cardamom, and salt to combine.

In a large bowl, use an electric mixer to beat the butter, cream cheese, sugar, and zest on medium-high speed until smooth and well combined, 1 to 2 minutes. Add the egg and beat until combined. On low speed, gradually add the flour mixture and beat until combined.

Scoop the dough into 2 tablespoon–sized balls and place on prepared baking sheets. Flatten with the bottom of a measuring cup to a 2-inch diameter.

Bake for 10 to 12 minutes, or until the cookies are set and begin to brown, rotating sheets halfway through. Let the cookies cool on the pan for 5 minutes before removing to a wire rack to cool completely. Freeze the cookies until frozen, at least 1 hour. Cookies can be stored in airtight containers in the freezer for up to 1 month.

**TO ASSEMBLE,** top one cookie with a scoop of ice cream. Place another cookie on top of the ice cream and gently press down to form a sandwich. Repeat for remaining cookies. Freeze for at least 1 hour, or until firm.

# Mango-Lime Ice Cream Sandwich

*Mango and lime work beautifully together to create a positively refreshing and flavorsome dessert. Just one taste of the exotic, sweet mango paired with the tart lime flavor will have everyone asking for more. Be sure to choose fragrant, ripe mangoes that are heavy and slightly soft.*

## MANGO ICE CREAM

**MAKES ABOUT 1 QUART**

**2 ripe mangoes**
**1½ cups whole milk**
**1½ cups heavy cream**
**¾ cup granulated sugar, divided**
**¼ teaspoon fine sea salt**
**½ teaspoon vanilla extract**
**4 large egg yolks**
**1 tablespoon fresh lemon juice**

To make mango puree, slice both ends off the mangoes to create a flat base and reveal the pit inside. Remove the skin and slice the fruit away from the pit. Place the mango fruit in a food processor or blender and puree until smooth. Mango puree can be stored in an airtight container in the refrigerator for up to 3 days. If using right away, set aside.

Prepare an ice bath by filling a large bowl with ice cubes and 1 to 2 cups of water. Place a medium bowl fitted with a fine strainer inside the ice bath.

In a medium saucepan, combine the milk, cream, ½ cup sugar, salt, and vanilla. Set over medium heat, stirring occasionally, until the mixture is warm and begins to steam, about 5 minutes.

In a medium bowl, whisk together the egg yolks and the remaining ¼ cup sugar. Carefully whisk half of the warm milk mixture into the egg yolks, one ladleful at a time, until the egg mixture is warmed. Whisk the egg-milk mixture back into the saucepan. Cook the mixture over medium heat, stirring constantly with a wooden spoon, until the mixture is thick enough to coat the back of the spoon and registers around 175°F on an instant-read thermometer, about 5 to 7 minutes. Be careful not to boil the mixture. Remove from the heat and stir in the mango puree and lemon juice.

Strain the mixture through a fine strainer into the prepared ice bath. Cool the custard in the ice bath until it reaches room temperature, stirring often. Press plastic wrap against the surface of the custard and refrigerate until chilled, about 4 hours or up to 1 day.

Pour the custard into an ice cream maker. Freeze according to the manufacturer's directions. Transfer to an airtight container, press plastic wrap against the ice cream surface, and freeze until it is firm and the flavor is ripened, at least 2 hours.

## GINGER-LIME COOKIES

**MAKES ABOUT 18 COOKIES**

**2 cups all-purpose flour**
**1 teaspoon ground ginger**
**½ teaspoon baking soda**
**¼ teaspoon fine sea salt**
**5 ounces (1¼ sticks) unsalted butter, at room temperature**
**¾ cup granulated sugar**
**Zest and juice from 2 large limes**
**1 large egg**
**½ teaspoon vanilla extract**

Preheat the oven to 350° F. Line large baking sheets with parchment paper or silicone baking mats.

In a medium bowl, whisk together the flour, ginger, baking soda, and salt.

In a large bowl, use an electric mixer to beat the butter and sugar on medium-high speed until smooth and well combined, about 1 to 2 minutes. Add the lime zest, lime juice, egg, and vanilla and beat until combined. On low speed, gradually add the flour mixture and beat until combined.

Roll the dough into 2 tablespoon–sized balls and place on prepared baking sheets. Flatten with the bottom of a measuring cup.

Bake for 10 minutes, or until the cookies are set and begin to brown. Let the cookies cool on the pan for 5 minutes, then remove to a wire rack to cool completely. Freeze the cookies until frozen, at least 1 hour. Cookies can be stored in airtight containers in the freezer for up to 1 month.

**TO ASSEMBLE,** top one cookie with a scoop of ice cream. Place another cookie on top of the ice cream and gently press down to form a sandwich. Repeat for remaining cookies. Freeze for at least 1 hour before serving.

# Strawberry Balsamic Ice Cream Sandwich

*Have you ever roasted strawberries before? If not, you must try it. It may seem strange to roast a fruit like strawberries, but it completely intensifies the flavor and transforms them into soft candylike gems. The aroma alone is intoxicating. When tangy balsamic roasted strawberries are added to creamy ice cream, it's paradise.*

## ROASTED STRAWBERRY ICE CREAM

### MAKES ABOUT 1 QUART

**2 pints fresh strawberries, hulled and quartered**

**3/4 cup granulated sugar, divided**

**2 tablespoons balsamic vinegar**

**1 cup whole milk**

**2 cups heavy cream**

**1/4 teaspoon fine sea salt**

**1/2 teaspoon vanilla extract**

**4 large egg yolks**

**1 tablespoon vodka**

Preheat the oven to 300°F. Line a large rimmed baking sheet with parchment paper.

Toss the strawberries with 1/4 cup sugar and the balsamic vinegar. Spread the strawberries into one even layer on the prepared baking sheet and roast for about 30 minutes, or until the strawberries have darkened in color and are soft and their juices have released. Transfer the strawberries to a medium bowl and mash until only small pieces of fruit remain. Cover and refrigerate the strawberries until chilled, about 1 hour.

Prepare an ice bath by filling a large bowl with ice cubes and 1 to 2 cups of water. Place a medium bowl fitted with a fine strainer inside the ice bath.

In a medium saucepan, combine the remaining 1/2 cup sugar, with the milk, cream, salt, and vanilla. Set over medium heat, stirring occasionally, until the mixture is warm and begins to steam, about 5 minutes.

Whisk together the egg yolks until well combined and pale in color. Carefully whisk half of the warm milk mixture into the egg yolks, until the egg mixture is warmed. Whisk the egg-milk mixture back into the saucepan. Cook the mixture over medium heat, stirring constantly, until the mixture is thick enough to coat the back of the spoon and registers around 175°F, about 5 to 7 minutes. Be careful not to boil the mixture.

Immediately strain the mixture through the fine strainer into the prepared ice bath. Cool the custard in the ice bath, stirring often. Press plastic wrap against the custard and refrigerate until chilled, about 4 hours or up to 1 day.

Pour the custard into an ice cream maker. Freeze according to the manufacturer's directions. During the last 5 minutes of freezing, add the roasted strawberries and vodka. Transfer the ice cream to an airtight container, press plastic wrap against the ice cream, and freeze, at least 2 hours.

# CHOCOLATE BALSAMIC COOKIES

**MAKES ABOUT 18 COOKIES**

**1 cup all-purpose flour**

**$^1/_3$ cup unsweetened cocoa powder**

**1 teaspoon baking powder**

**$^1/_4$ teaspoon fine sea salt**

**5 ounces (1$^1/_4$ sticks) unsalted butter, at room temperature**

**$^1/_4$ cup packed light brown sugar**

**$^3/_4$ cup granulated sugar**

**1 large egg**

**$^1/_4$ teaspoon vanilla extract**

**2 tablespoons balsamic vinegar**

**4 ounces bittersweet chocolate, chopped**

Preheat the oven to 350°F. Line baking sheets with parchment paper. In a medium bowl, sift together the flour, cocoa powder, baking powder, and salt.

In a large bowl, beat the butter and sugars on medium-high speed until smooth, about 1 to 2 minutes. Add the egg, vanilla, and balsamic vinegar and beat until combined. On low speed, gradually add the flour mixture until combined. Fold in the chopped chocolate with a rubber spatula.

Using a spoon or spring-loaded scoop, drop 2 tablespoon–sized balls of dough onto prepared baking sheets.

Bake for about 10 minutes, or until the cookies are set. Let cool completely. Freeze the cookies until frozen, at least 1 hour. Cookies can be stored in airtight containers in the freezer for up to 1 month.

**TO ASSEMBLE,** top one cookie with a scoop of ice cream. Place another cookie on top and gently press down to form a sandwich. Repeat for the remaining cookies. Freeze for at least 1 hour before serving.

# Lemon-Blueberry Ice Cream Sandwich

*The combination of fresh Blueberry Ice Cream with sweet and tart Lemon Cookies tastes like a beautiful summer day with every bite. Not only does this sandwich taste wonderful, but it also looks just as great. The ice cream is a brilliant violet color, and you can actually see flecks of yellow lemon zest in the cookies. Make these for your next summer cookout—they're sure to be a hit.*

## BLUEBERRY ICE CREAM

### MAKES ABOUT 1½ QUARTS

**4 cups fresh blueberries**
**1 tablespoon fresh lemon juice**
**1 cup granulated sugar, divided**
**1 cup whole milk**
**2 cups heavy cream**
**¼ teaspoon fine sea salt**
**1 teaspoon vanilla extract**
**4 large egg yolks**
**1 tablespoon vodka**

To make blueberry puree, place the blueberries, lemon juice, and ¾ cup sugar in a large saucepan set over medium-high heat. Bring the mixture to a boil, then reduce heat to a simmer and cook, stirring often, until the sugar is dissolved and the berries are soft, about 7 minutes. Let cool slightly, then carefully puree the mixture in a blender or food processor until smooth, about 30 seconds to 2 minutes. Strain the mixture through a fine strainer to remove seeds and skins. Blueberry puree can be stored in an airtight container in the refrigerator for up to 3 days. If using right away, set aside.

Prepare an ice bath by filling a large bowl with ice cubes and 1 to 2 cups of water. Place a medium bowl fitted with a fine strainer inside the ice bath.

In a clean medium saucepan, combine the blueberry puree, milk, cream, salt, and vanilla. Set over medium heat, stirring occasionally, until the mixture is warm and begins to steam, about 5 minutes.

In a medium bowl, whisk together the egg yolks and the remaining ¼ cup sugar. Carefully whisk half of the warm milk mixture into the egg yolks, one ladleful at a time, until the egg mixture is warmed. Whisk the egg-milk mixture back into the saucepan. Cook the mixture over medium heat, stirring constantly, until the mixture is thick enough to coat the back of the spoon and registers around 175°F on an instant-read thermometer, about 5 to 7 minutes. Be careful not to boil the mixture.

Immediately strain the mixture through the fine strainer into the prepared ice bath. Cool the custard in the ice bath, stirring often. Press plastic wrap against the surface of the custard and refrigerate until chilled, about 4 hours or up to 1 day.

Pour the custard into an ice cream maker. Freeze according to the manufacturer's directions. During the last minute of freezing, add the vodka. Transfer to an airtight container, press plastic wrap against the ice cream, and freeze until it is firm, at least 2 hours.

# LEMON COOKIES

**MAKES ABOUT 20 COOKIES**

2¼ **cups all-purpose flour**
¼ **teaspoon fine sea salt**
¼ **teaspoon baking soda**
8 **ounces (2 sticks) unsalted butter, at room temperature**
1 **cup granulated sugar**
**Zest and juice from 2 large lemons**
1 **large egg**
1 **teaspoon vanilla extract**

Preheat the oven to 350°F. Line large baking sheets with parchment paper or silicone baking mats.

In a medium bowl, whisk together the flour, salt, and baking soda.

In a large bowl, beat the butter and sugar on medium-high speed until smooth, about 1 to 2 minutes. Add the lemon zest and juice, beating until combined. Add the egg and vanilla and beat until combined. On low speed, gradually add the flour mixture and beat until combined.

Scoop the dough into 2 tablespoon–sized balls and place on prepared baking sheets.

Bake for about 10 minutes, or until the cookies are set and begin to brown at the edges. Let the cookies cool completely. Freeze the cookies until frozen, at least 1 hour. Cookies can be stored in airtight containers in the freezer for up to 1 month.

**TO ASSEMBLE,** top one cookie with a scoop of ice cream. Place another cookie on top and gently press down to form a sandwich. Repeat for remaining cookies. Freeze for at least 1 hour before serving.

# Peaches and Cream Ice Cream Sandwich

### MAKES ABOUT 9 ICE CREAM SANDWICHES

*You practically get an entire serving of fruit with each of these fresh ice cream sandwiches. The next time you see perfect peaches at the fruit stand, be sure to make a batch of these. You won't regret it.*

## PEACH ICE CREAM

### MAKES ABOUT 1½ QUARTS

**1 pound fresh ripe or thawed frozen peaches, peeled, pitted, and chopped**
**2 tablespoons fresh lemon juice**
**1 cup granulated sugar, divided**
**1½ cups whole milk**
**1½ cups heavy cream**
**¼ teaspoon fine sea salt**
**½ teaspoon vanilla extract**
**5 large egg yolks**
**1 tablespoon vodka**

To make peach puree, combine the peaches, lemon juice, and ½ cup sugar in a medium bowl. Let the mixture macerate for 2 hours. Mash the mixture with a potato masher or fork until only small pieces of fruit remain. Transfer to an air-tight container and refrigerate until chilled, or up to 2 days.

Prepare an ice bath by filling a large bowl with ice cubes and 1 to 2 cups of water. Place a medium bowl fitted with a fine strainer inside the ice bath.

In a medium saucepan, combine ¼ cup sugar, milk, cream, salt, and vanilla. Set over medium heat, stirring occasionally, until the mixture is warm and begins to steam, about 5 minutes.

In a medium bowl, whisk together the egg yolks and the remaining ¼ cup sugar. Carefully whisk half of the warm milk mixture into the egg yolks, one ladleful at a time, until the egg mixture is warmed. Whisk the egg-milk mixture back into the saucepan. Cook the mixture over medium heat, stirring constantly with a wooden spoon, until the mixture is thick enough to coat the back of the spoon and registers around 175°F on an instant-read thermometer, about 5 to 7 minutes. Be careful not to boil the mixture.

Strain the mixture through the fine strainer into the prepared ice bath. Stir in the peach puree. Cool the custard in the ice bath until it reaches room temperature, stirring often. Press plastic wrap against the surface of the custard and refrigerate until chilled, about 4 hours or up to 1 day.

Pour the custard into an ice cream maker. Freeze according to the manufacturer's directions. During the last minute of freezing, add the vodka. Transfer to an airtight container, press plastic wrap against the ice cream surface, and freeze until it is firm and the flavor is ripened, at least 2 hours.

# CINNAMON HONEY COOKIES

**MAKES ABOUT 18 COOKIES**

**2 cups all-purpose flour**

**$^1/_2$ teaspoon baking soda**

**$^1/_4$ teaspoon baking powder**

**$^1/_2$ teaspoon ground cinnamon, plus more for sprinkling**

**$^1/_4$ teaspoon fine sea salt**

**4 ounces (1 stick) unsalted butter, at room temperature**

**$^1/_2$ cup packed light brown sugar**

**$^1/_2$ cup honey**

**1 large egg**

Preheat the oven to 350°F. Line baking sheets with parchment paper or silicone baking mats.

In a medium bowl, whisk together the flour, baking soda, baking powder, cinnamon, and salt.

In a large bowl, use an electric mixer to beat the butter and sugar on medium-high speed until well combined and smooth, about 1 to 2 minutes. Add the honey and egg and beat until combined. On low speed, gradually add the flour mixture.

Using a spoon or spring-loaded scoop, drop 2 tablespoon–sized balls of dough onto prepared baking sheets.

Bake for about 8 to 10 minutes, or until the edges are slightly browned. Let cool on baking sheets for 5 minutes before removing to wire racks to cool completely. Freeze the cookies until frozen, at least 1 hour. Cookies can be stored in airtight containers in the freezer for up to 1 month.

**TO ASSEMBLE,** top one cookie with a scoop of ice cream. Place another cookie on top of the ice cream and gently press down to form a sandwich. Sprinkle the edges of the sandwich with cinnamon, if desired. Repeat for the remaining cookies. Freeze for at least 1 hour before serving.

# Sinful

THIS CHAPTER IS LADEN WITH OVER-THE-TOP DELECTABLE INDULGENCES. From The Elvis Ice Cream Sandwich, which includes bacon, to the Birthday Cake Ice Cream Sandwich, which includes cake batter, the sandwiches in this chapter may be the best you will ever have. These sandwiches look as mouthwatering as they taste, so try not to get any drool on the photos!

There's a Red Velvet Sandwich and a Cinnamon Roll Sandwich. There's even chocolate chip cookie dough, brown butter, and dulce de leche. It doesn't get much better than these ingredients and flavors. I know you will have a blast with these spectacular recipes, and I hope you savor each bite.

# The Elvis Ice Cream Sandwich

*You can also call this sandwich "The King," because it may be one of the most over-the-top-indulgent treats ever. Thick, rich, and nutty Peanut Butter Ice Cream is paired with soft Banana Oat Cookies. The best part, however, is the crumbled bacon around the edges. One bite will have you talking like Elvis: "Thank you, thank you very much."*

## PEANUT BUTTER ICE CREAM

### MAKES ABOUT 1 QUART

**1 cup peanut butter, smooth or chunky**
**1½ cups whole milk**
**1½ cups heavy cream**
**¾ cup granulated sugar, divided**
**¼ teaspoon fine sea salt**
**1 teaspoon vanilla extract**
**4 large egg yolks**

Prepare an ice bath by filling a large bowl with ice cubes and 1 to 2 cups of water. Place a medium bowl fitted with a fine strainer inside the ice bath.

In a medium saucepan set over medium heat, melt the peanut butter until thinned and smooth. Add the milk, cream, ½ cup sugar, salt, and vanilla, and stir. Cook for another 2 to 3 minutes, or until the mixture is warmed.

In a medium bowl, whisk together the egg yolks and the remaining ¼ cup sugar. Carefully whisk half of the warm milk mixture into the egg yolks, one ladleful at a time, until the egg mixture is warmed. Whisk the egg-milk mixture back into the saucepan. Cook the mixture over medium heat, stirring constantly with a wooden spoon, until the mixture is thick enough to coat the back of the spoon and registers around 175°F on an instant-read thermometer, about 5 to 7 minutes. Be careful not to boil the mixture.

Immediately strain the mixture through the fine strainer into the prepared ice bath. Cool the custard in the ice bath until it reaches room temperature, stirring often. Press plastic wrap against the surface of the custard and refrigerate until chilled, about 4 hours or up to 1 day.

Pour the chilled mixture into an ice cream maker. Freeze according to the manufacturer's directions. Transfer the ice cream to an air-tight container, press plastic wrap against the ice cream surface, and freeze until it is firm and the flavor is ripened, at least 2 hours.

## BANANA OAT COOKIES

**MAKES ABOUT 22 COOKIES**

**2 cups all-purpose flour**
**1 cup old-fashioned rolled oats**
**$^{1}/_{2}$ teaspoon baking soda**
**$^{1}/_{4}$ teaspoon fine sea salt**
**5 ounces ($1^{1}/_{4}$ sticks) unsalted butter, melted and cooled**
**$^{1}/_{4}$ cup granulated sugar**
**$^{3}/_{4}$ cup packed light brown sugar**
**1 large egg**
**1 large egg yolk**
**2 medium ripe bananas, mashed (about 1 cup)**
**1 teaspoon vanilla extract**
**$^{1}/_{2}$ teaspoon ground cinnamon**

Preheat the oven to 350°F. Line baking sheets with parchment paper or silicone baking mats.

In a small bowl, whisk together the flour, oats, baking soda, and salt.

In a large bowl, mix the butter and sugars with a rubber spatula. Add the egg and egg yolk, stirring to combine. Stir in the mashed bananas, vanilla, and cinnamon. The mixture will be lumpy. Gradually add the flour mixture and stir until everything is thoroughly combined.

Using a spoon or spring-loaded scoop, drop 2 tablespoon–sized balls of dough onto pre-pared baking sheets. Flatten slightly with the palm of your hand. Chill the dough in the refrigerator for 30 minutes.

Bake for about 11 to 12 minutes, or until the edges are slightly browned. Let cool on baking sheets for 5 minutes before removing to wire racks to cool completely. Freeze the cookies until frozen, at least 1 hour. Cookies can be stored in airtight containers in the freezer for up to 1 month.

### For Decorating:

**4 strips of bacon, crisp-cooked and crumbled, for rolling**

**TO ASSEMBLE,** place the bacon in a shallow dish. Top one cookie with a scoop of ice cream. Place another cookie on top of the ice cream and gently press down to form a sand-wich, allowing the ice cream to ooze out the sides slightly. Roll the edges in the crumbled bacon. Immediately place the sandwich in the freezer. Repeat for the remaining sandwiches. Freeze the sandwiches until firm, at least 1 hour, before serving.

# Red Velvet Ice Cream Sandwich

*Say "red velvet," and suddenly everyone is listening, mouths watering ever so slightly. However, you don't know how good red velvet can be until you've tried this sandwich, which pairs tangy and rich Cream Cheese Ice Cream with brilliantly colored and beautifully shaped red velvet cutout cookies. These sandwiches are the perfect dessert for many occasions throughout the year.*

## CREAM CHEESE ICE CREAM

### MAKES ABOUT 1 QUART

**8 ounces cream cheese,**
  **at room temperature**
**1¼ cups whole milk**
**1¼ cups heavy cream**
**¾ cup granulated sugar**
**Pinch of fine sea salt**
**1½ teaspoons vanilla extract**

In the work bowl of a blender or food processor, puree the cream cheese, milk, cream, sugar, salt, and vanilla until smooth, scraping down the sides of the bowl as necessary. Transfer the mixture to a medium bowl and press plastic wrap against the surface. Refrigerate until completely chilled, at least 30 minutes.

Pour the chilled mixture into the ice cream maker. Freeze according to the manufacturer's directions. Line a large rimmed baking pan (or another similar large, flat container) with parchment paper or plastic wrap. Spread the freshly churned ice cream evenly over the lined baking sheet. Press additional plastic wrap against the surface of the ice cream. Freeze until totally firm, at least 2 hours or up to 3 days. The longer you freeze it, the easier it will be to form the ice cream sandwiches.

## RED VELVET COOKIES

### MAKES ABOUT 24 COOKIES

**3 cups all-purpose flour,**
  **plus more for dusting**
**¼ cup unsweetened cocoa powder**
**2½ teaspoons baking powder**
**Pinch of fine sea salt**

**6 ounces (1½ sticks) unsalted butter, at room temperature**

**1½ cups granulated sugar**

**2 large eggs**

**2 teaspoons pure vanilla extract**

**1 teaspoon red gel food coloring**

In a medium bowl, sift together the flour, cocoa powder, baking powder, and salt.

In a large bowl, use an electric mixer to beat the butter and sugar for 2 minutes, or until well combined and smooth. Add the eggs, one at a time, until combined. Add the vanilla extract and food coloring and continue beating until thoroughly combined. On low speed, add the flour mixture and beat until combined. Wrap the dough in plastic wrap and chill in the refrigerator until firm, about 1 hour or up to 2 days.

Line large baking sheets with parchment paper or silicone baking mats. Place the chilled dough in between two large pieces of parchment paper or plastic wrap on a work surface. Roll the dough to a ¼-inch thickness. If the dough is too firm, let it sit at room temperature for 5 to 10 minutes before rolling. Using a tall round cookie cutter, carefully cut out rounds from the dough and place on the prepared baking sheets. Chill the baking sheets in the refrigerator for 30 minutes or until firm.

Preheat the oven to 350°F.

Remove the baking sheets from refrigerator and prick the dough squares all over with the end of an instant-read thermometer or skewer. Bake for 10 to 11 minutes, or until the cookies are set. Let cool on baking sheets for 5 minutes before removing to a wire rack to cool completely. Freeze the cookies until frozen, at least 1 hour. Cookies can be stored in airtight containers in the freezer for up to 1 month.

**TO ASSEMBLE,** remove the ice cream sheet from the freezer. Using the same cookie cutter, cut out a round of ice cream and sandwich it between two cookies. Repeat for remaining cookies, working quickly. If the ice cream begins to melt, return it to the freezer until it is firm again. Freeze the sandwiches until firm, at least 1 hour, before serving.

*Tip:* For a special Valentine's Day treat, cut these sandwiches into big heart shapes.

# Cinnamon Roll Ice Cream Sandwich

*Want your house to smell better than any candle? Bake up a batch of these Cinnamon Roll Cookies, which are as tasty as they are pretty. The Brown Butter Ice Cream adds an easy gourmet twist to this indulgent, fun, and gorgeous dessert.*

## BROWN BUTTER ICE CREAM

### MAKES ABOUT 1 QUART

**4 ounces (1 stick) unsalted butter**
**1½ cups whole milk**
**1½ cups heavy cream**
**¼ teaspoon fine sea salt**
**⅓ cup granulated sugar**
**⅓ cup packed light brown sugar**
**4 large egg yolks**

Prepare an ice bath by filling a large bowl with ice cubes and 1 to 2 cups of water. Place a medium bowl fitted with a fine strainer inside the ice bath.

In a small skillet set over medium-low heat, melt the butter. Continue to cook the butter, swirling the pan occasionally, until it develops a deep amber color, about 8 to 10 minutes. Remove from heat.

In a medium saucepan, combine the milk, cream, salt, and granulated sugar. Set over medium heat, stirring occasionally, until the mixture is warm and begins to steam, about 5 minutes.

In a medium bowl, whisk together the brown sugar, yolks, and brown butter until thick and well combined. Carefully whisk half of the warm milk mixture into the egg yolks, one ladleful at a time, until the egg mixture is warmed. Whisk the egg-milk mixture back into the saucepan. Cook the mixture over medium heat, stirring constantly, until the mixture is thick enough to coat the back of the spoon and registers around 175°F, about 5 minutes. Be careful not to boil the mixture.

Immediately strain the mixture through the fine strainer into the prepared ice bath. Cool the custard in the ice bath, stirring often. Press plastic wrap against the custard and refrigerate until chilled, about 4 hours or up to 1 day.

Pour the chilled mixture into an ice cream maker. Freeze according to the manufacturer's directions. Transfer the ice cream to an airtight container, press plastic wrap against the ice cream, and freeze, at least 2 hours or up to 3 days.

# CINNAMON ROLL COOKIES

### MAKES ABOUT 24 COOKIES

*For the cookies:*
**1½ cups all-purpose flour**
**1 teaspoon baking powder**
**¼ teaspoon fine sea salt**
**6 ounces (1½ sticks) unsalted butter, at room temperature**
**¾ cup granulated sugar**
**1 large egg**
**1 teaspoon vanilla extract**

*For the filling:*
**2 tablespoons unsalted butter, melted**
**2 tablespoons granulated sugar**
**2 tablespoons packed light brown sugar**
**1 tablespoon ground cinnamon**

In a small bowl, whisk together the flour, baking powder, and salt.

In a large bowl, beat the butter and sugar on medium-high speed until smooth. Add the egg and vanilla and beat until combined. On low speed, gradually add the flour mixture,

beating until combined.

Shape the dough into a flat disk, wrap it in plastic, and chill in the refrigerator until firm, at least 2 hours.

For the filling, place the dough in between two large sheets of parchment paper. Roll the dough out into a large ¼-inch-thick rectangle. Brush the dough with the melted butter. In a small bowl, combine the sugars and cinnamon. Sprinkle mixture evenly over the dough.

With the long side facing you, gently roll the dough into a log, using the parchment paper to guide the dough and prevent sticking. Wrap in parchment paper and freeze until firm, about 20 to 30 minutes.

Preheat the oven to 375°F. Line large baking sheets with parchment paper.

Once the log is firm, use a sharp knife to gently cut ½-inch slices of dough. Place the slices on prepared baking sheets and bake for 10 to 12 minutes, or until the edges are lightly golden. Let cool completely. Freeze the cookies until frozen, at least 1 hour. Cookies can be stored in airtight containers in the freezer for up to 1 month.

**TO ASSEMBLE,** top one cookie with a scoop of ice cream. Place another cookie on top and gently press down to form a sandwich. Freeze for at least 1 hour before serving.

# Birthday Cake Ice Cream Sandwich

*Serve this ice cream sandwich to your kids, grandkids, nieces or nephews, cousins, siblings, or friends, and they will love you. The Cake Batter Ice Cream tastes exactly like frozen cake batter. Plus, who doesn't love Funfetti Cookies? This ice cream sandwich recipe uses a ridiculous amount of sprinkles, so you know it's bound to be great.*

## CAKE BATTER ICE CREAM

**MAKES ABOUT 1 QUART**

1½ **cups whole milk**
1½ **cups heavy cream**
½ **cup granulated sugar**
½ **cup yellow cake mix, sifted**
¼ **teaspoon fine sea salt**
1 **teaspoon vanilla extract**
4 **large egg yolks**

Prepare an ice bath by filling a large bowl with ice cubes and 1 to 2 cups of water. Place a medium bowl fitted with a fine strainer inside the ice bath.

In a medium saucepan, combine the milk, cream, sugar, cake mix, salt, and vanilla. Set over medium heat, stirring occasionally, until the mixture is warm and begins to steam, about 5 minutes.

In a medium bowl, whisk the egg yolks until smooth. Carefully whisk half of the warm milk mixture into the egg yolks, one ladleful at a time, until the egg mixture is warmed. Whisk the egg-milk mixture back into the saucepan. Cook the mixture over medium heat, stirring constantly with a wooden spoon, until the mixture is thick enough to coat the back of the spoon and registers around 175°F on an instant-read thermometer, about 5 to 7 minutes. Be careful not to boil the mixture.

Immediately strain the mixture through the fine strainer into the medium bowl set over the ice bath. Cool the custard in the ice bath until it reaches room temperature, stirring often. Press plastic wrap against the surface of the custard and refrigerate until chilled, about 4 hours or up to 1 day.

Pour the chilled mixture into an ice cream maker. Freeze according to the manufacturer's directions. Transfer the ice cream to an airtight container, press plastic wrap against the ice cream surface, and freeze until it is firm and the flavor is ripened, at least 2 hours.

# FUNFETTI COOKIES

**MAKES ABOUT 18 COOKIES**

1³/₄ **cups all-purpose flour**
³/₄ **teaspoon baking powder**
¹/₄ **teaspoon baking soda**
¹/₄ **teaspoon fine sea salt**
4 **ounces (1 stick) unsalted butter,**
  **at room temperature**
³/₄ **cup granulated sugar**
1 **tablespoon milk**
1 **large egg**
¹/₂ **teaspoon vanilla extract**
¹/₄ **teaspoon almond extract**
¹/₂ **cup rainbow sprinkles**

Preheat the oven to 350° F. Line large baking sheets with parchment paper or silicone baking mats.

In a medium bowl, whisk the flour, baking powder, baking soda, and salt to combine.

In a large bowl, use an electric mixer to beat the butter and sugar on medium-high speed until well combined and smooth, about 1 to 2 minutes. Add the milk, egg, and extracts and beat until combined. On low speed, gradually add the flour mixture and beat until combined. Mix in the sprinkles with a rubber spatula until combined.

Using a spoon or spring-loaded scoop, drop 2 tablespoon–sized balls of dough onto prepared baking sheets.

Bake for 10 to 12 minutes, or until the cookies are set and begin to brown at the edges. Let the cookies cool on the pan for 5 minutes, then remove to a wire rack to cool completely. Freeze the cookies until frozen, at least 1 hour. Cookies can be stored in airtight containers in the freezer for up to 1 month.

## For Decorating:

**Rainbow sprinkles (about ¹/₂ cup),**
  **for rolling**

**TO ASSEMBLE,** place the sprinkles in a shallow dish. Top one cookie with a scoop of ice cream. Place another cookie on top of the ice cream and gently press down to form a sandwich. Roll the edges in sprinkles. Immediately place the sandwich in the freezer. Repeat for the remaining cookies. Freeze sandwiches for at least 1 hour before serving.

# Salty-Sweet Ice Cream Sandwich

*One of my hands-down favorite flavor combinations is salty and sweet. When you put Salted Caramel Ice Cream and Bacon Chocolate Chip Cookies together, you have the ultimate salty-sweet confection. Don't worry: This recipe manages to perfectly balance the saltiness with the sweetness for ultimate satisfaction.*

## SALTED CARAMEL ICE CREAM

**MAKES ABOUT 1½ QUARTS**

**1¼ cups granulated sugar**
**4 tablespoons unsalted butter**
**1½ cups heavy cream**
**1½ cups whole milk**
**4 large egg yolks**
**1 tablespoon vanilla extract**
**¾ teaspoon fine sea salt**

Prepare an ice bath by filling a large bowl with ice cubes and 1 to 2 cups of water. Place a medium bowl fitted with a fine strainer inside the ice bath.

In a medium dry saucepan, cook the sugar over medium heat, swirling the pan occasionally, until it melts and begins to turn a deep golden color, about 5 minutes. Carefully add the butter, cream, and milk to the pot (be cautious: the mixture may splatter). The caramel may seize but will melt as it's heated. Reduce heat slightly and cook until the mixture is smooth and just simmering, about 1 to 5 minutes (or longer if the caramel seized). Remove from heat.

In a medium bowl, whisk the egg yolks until smooth and light in color. Carefully whisk half of the warm milk mixture into the egg yolks, one ladleful at a time, until the egg mixture is warmed. Whisk the egg-milk mixture back into the saucepan. Cook the mixture over medium heat, stirring constantly, until the mixture is thick enough to coat the back of the spoon and registers around 175°F, about 5 to 7 minutes. Be careful not to boil the mixture.

Immediately strain the mixture through the fine strainer into the prepared ice bath. Stir in the vanilla and salt. Cool the custard in the ice bath until it reaches room temperature, stirring often. Press plastic wrap against the custard and refrigerate until chilled, about 4 hours or up to 1 day.

Pour the chilled custard into an ice cream maker. Freeze according to the manufacturer's directions. Transfer the ice cream to an airtight container, press plastic wrap against the ice cream, and freeze until it is firm, at least 3 hours.

# BACON CHOCOLATE CHIP COOKIES

**MAKES ABOUT 18 COOKIES**

1¼ **cups all-purpose flour**

½ **teaspoon baking soda**

¼ **teaspoon baking powder**

¼ **teaspoon fine sea salt**

4 **ounces (1 stick) unsalted butter, at room temperature**

½ **cup granulated sugar**

½ **cup packed light brown sugar**

1 **large egg**

1 **tablespoon milk**

1 **teaspoon vanilla extract**

5 **slices crisp-cooked bacon, crumbled**

½ **cup semisweet chocolate chips**

Preheat the oven to 350°F. Line baking sheets with parchment paper or silicone baking mats.

In a medium bowl, whisk together the flour, baking soda, baking powder, and salt.

In a large bowl, use an electric mixer to beat the butter and sugars on medium-high speed until light and smooth, about 1 to 2 minutes. Beat in the egg, milk, and vanilla. Gradually add the flour mixture and beat until combined. Fold in the crumbled bacon and chocolate chips with a rubber spatula.

Using a spoon or spring-loaded scoop, drop 2 tablespoon–sized balls of dough onto prepared baking sheets. Flatten slightly with the palm of your hand.

Bake for about 10 to 12 minutes, or until the edges are slightly browned. Let cool completely. Freeze the cookies until frozen, at least 1 hour. Cookies can be stored in airtight containers in the freezer for up to 1 month.

## For decorating:

**Chopped semisweet chocolate (about 4 ounces), for rolling**

**TO ASSEMBLE,** place the chopped chocolate in a shallow dish. Top one cookie with a scoop of ice cream. Place another cookie on top of the ice cream and gently press down to form a sandwich. Roll the edges in the chopped chocolate and repeat for the remaining cookies. Freeze for at least 1 hour before serving.

# Brookie Ice Cream Sandwich

*You're probably asking yourself, what in the world is a brookie? Well, it's nothing short of a dessert miracle. A brookie is a brownie in cookie form. This chocolate treat is fudgelike, with that crinkled top just like a brownie. However, it is also slightly crisp at the edges and perfectly round. When sandwiching Chocolate Chip Cookie Dough Ice Cream, every bite will feel like a taste of heaven.*

## CHOCOLATE CHIP COOKIE DOUGH ICE CREAM

**MAKES ABOUT 1½ QUARTS**

*For the cookie dough:*
**4 tablespoons unsalted butter, melted**
**1 tablespoon whole milk**
**½ teaspoon vanilla extract**
**⅓ cup packed light brown sugar**
**⅔ cup all-purpose flour**
**Pinch of fine sea salt**
**½ cup miniature semisweet chocolate chips**

*For the ice cream:*
**1½ cups whole milk**
**1½ cups heavy cream**
**½ cup granulated sugar**
**¼ teaspoon fine sea salt**
**½ teaspoon vanilla extract**
**4 large egg yolks**

**FOR THE COOKIE DOUGH:** In a medium bowl, combine the butter, milk, vanilla, and sugar with a rubber spatula. Stir in the flour and salt. Fold in the chocolate chips. Pat the dough into a flat disk and wrap in plastic wrap. Refrigerate until firm, about 1 hour.

Once the dough is firm, chop it into small chunks. Place the cookie dough in the freezer until ready to use.

**FOR THE ICE CREAM:** Prepare an ice bath by filling a large bowl with ice cubes and 1 to 2 cups of water. Place a medium bowl fitted with a fine strainer inside the ice bath.

In a medium saucepan, combine the milk, cream, sugar, salt, and vanilla. Set over medium heat, stirring occasionally, until the mixture is warm and begins to steam, about 5 minutes.

In a small bowl, whisk the egg yolks until smooth and light in color. Carefully whisk half of the warm milk mixture into the egg yolks, one ladleful at a time, until the egg mixture is warmed. Whisk the egg-milk mixture back into the saucepan. Cook the mixture over medium heat, stirring constantly, until the mixture is thick enough to coat the back of the spoon, about 5 to 7 minutes. Be careful not to boil the mixture.

Immediately strain the mixture through the fine strainer into the ice bath. Cool the custard in the ice bath, stirring often. Press plastic wrap against the custard and refrigerate until chilled, about 4 hours or up to 1 day.

Pour the mixture into an ice cream maker. Freeze according to the manufacturer's directions. Remove the ice cream to an airtight container and fold in the cookie dough. Press plastic wrap against the ice cream, and freeze, at least 2 hours.

## BROOKIES

**MAKES ABOUT 18 COOKIES**

**¹/₂ cup all-purpose flour**
**3 tablespoons unsweetened cocoa powder**
**¹/₄ teaspoon baking powder**
**¹/₄ teaspoon salt**
**12 ounces semisweet chocolate, chopped**
**4 tablespoons unsalted butter,**
  **at room temperature**

**3 large eggs**
**2 tablespoons milk**
**³/₄ cup granulated sugar**
**¹/₂ teaspoon vanilla extract**

In a medium bowl, sift together the flour, cocoa powder, baking powder, and salt.

Place the chocolate and butter in a large microwave-safe bowl. Microwave in 20-second bursts, stirring between bursts, until the mixture is melted and smooth. Let cool.

Add the eggs and milk to the chocolate mixture, stirring to combine. Add the sugar and vanilla and stir until combined. Stir in the flour mixture until smooth. Cover the batter with plastic wrap and refrigerate until the mixture is firm, about 1 hour.

Preheat the oven to 350°F. Line large baking sheets with parchment paper.

Drop 2 tablespoon–sized balls on prepared baking sheets, spacing 2 inches apart. Bake for 8 to 10 minutes, or until the tops of the cookies are cracked. Let cool completely. Freeze the cookies until frozen, at least 1 hour. Cookies can be stored in airtight containers in the freezer for up to 1 month.

**TO ASSEMBLE,** top one cookie with a scoop of ice cream. Place another cookie on top and gently press down to form a sandwich. Freeze for at least 1 hour before serving.

# Dulce de Leche Ice Cream Sandwich

*We should all thank South America for contributing dulce de leche to the world. The term translates to "candy of milk" and refers to a mixture of milk and sugar that is cooked until it reaches a caramel-like consistency and taste. Luckily, you can purchase it prepared in many grocery stores in the Latin food aisle. Just try not to eat all of it straight from the can.*

## DULCE DE LECHE ICE CREAM

### MAKES ABOUT 1 QUART

**1¹/₂ cups whole milk**
**1¹/₂ cups heavy cream**
**1 cup dulce de leche, divided**
**¹/₄ cup granulated sugar**
**¹/₂ teaspoon fine sea salt**
**4 large egg yolks**

Prepare an ice bath by filling a large bowl with ice cubes and 1 to 2 cups of water. Place a medium bowl fitted with a fine strainer inside the ice bath.

In a medium saucepan, combine the milk, cream, ¹/₂ cup dulce de leche, sugar, and salt. Set over medium heat, stirring occasionally, until the mixture is warm and begins to steam, about 5 minutes.

In a medium bowl, whisk together the egg yolks. Carefully whisk half of the warm milk mixture into the egg yolks, one ladleful at a time, until the egg mixture is warmed. Whisk the egg-milk mixture back into the saucepan. Cook the mixture over medium heat, stirring constantly with a wooden spoon, until the mixture is thick enough to coat the back of the spoon and registers around 175°F on an instant-read thermometer, about 5 to 7 minutes. Be careful not to boil the mixture.

Immediately strain the mixture through the fine strainer into the prepared ice bath. Cool the custard in the ice bath until it reaches room temperature, stirring often. Press plastic wrap against the surface of the custard and refrigerate until chilled, about 4 hours or up to 1 day.

Pour the chilled mixture into an ice cream maker. Freeze according to the manufacturer's directions. During the last minutes of freezing, pour the remaining ¹/₂ cup dulce de leche into the ice cream. If using a decorative cookie cutter to make the ice cream sandwiches, line a large rimmed baking sheet (or another large, flat container) with parchment paper or plastic wrap. Spread the freshly churned ice cream evenly over the lined baking sheet. Press additional plastic wrap against the surface of the ice cream. Freeze until firm, at least 3 hours or up to 3 days. Alternatively, transfer the ice cream to an airtight container, press plastic wrap against the ice cream surface, and freeze until it is firm and the flavor is ripened, at least 4 hours.

## CHOCOLATE SHORTBREAD COOKIES

**MAKES ABOUT 24 COOKIES**

**2 cups all-purpose flour**

**$1/2$ cup unsweetened cocoa powder**

**$1/4$ teaspoon fine sea salt**

**8 ounces (2 sticks) unsalted butter, at room temperature**

**1 cup confectioners' sugar**

In a medium bowl, sift together the flour, cocoa powder, and salt.

In a large bowl, use an electric mixer to beat the butter until smooth. Add the sugar and beat until well combined. On low speed, slowly add the flour mixture and beat until combined. Flatten the dough into a disk and wrap in plastic. Chill for at least 1 hour or until firm.

Preheat the oven to 350° F. Line large baking sheets with parchment paper or silicone baking mats.

Place the dough between two large sheets of parchment paper and roll the dough out into a $1/4$-inch thickness. Cut out shapes from the dough using a $2 1/2$-inch round cookie cutter. Place on prepared baking sheets and bake for about 10 minutes, or until set. Cool the sheets for 5 minutes before removing the cookies to wire racks to cool completely. Freeze the cookies until frozen, at least 1 hour. Cookies can be stored in airtight containers in the freezer for up to 1 month.

**TO ASSEMBLE,** if you're using a decorative cookie cutter, remove the ice cream sheet from the freezer. Using the same cookie cutter, cut out a round of ice cream and sandwich it between two frozen cookies. Press cookies together until the ice cream meets the edge of each cookie. Place in the freezer. Repeat for the remaining cookies, working quickly. If the ice cream begins to melt, return to the freezer until firm again. Alternatively, top one cookie with a scoop of ice cream. Place another cookie on top of the ice cream and gently press down to form a sandwich. Freeze sandwiches until firm, at least 1 hour, before serving.

# Boozy

**L**ET'S ADMIT IT: MOST THINGS IN LIFE ARE BETTER WITH A LITTLE SPLASH of booze. The ice cream sandwiches in this chapter are inspired by popular alcoholic drinks and flavor combinations. Although none of the ice cream sandwiches here have a high enough alcohol content to really affect you, they sure do taste good.

The alcohol not only adds flavor, but it also makes the ice creams ultra rich, smooth, and luxurious. Make sure you work quickly when assembling these sandwiches because the ice creams tend to melt faster. Also, the sandwiches may need a little extra freezer time to firm up. The wait will be worth it, though, when you take your first bite of a boozy ice cream sandwich!

# Chocolate Stout Ice Cream Sandwich

*Perfect for St. Patrick's Day, this super chocolaty ice cream sandwich has a slight hint of stout beer that works perfectly with the salty pretzels around the edges. A fantastically sweet and salty ice cream sandwich made from bar food? Who would have thought?*

## CHOCOLATE STOUT ICE CREAM

### MAKES ABOUT 1½ QUARTS

1¼ **cups whole milk**

1¼ **cups heavy cream**

1 **teaspoon vanilla extract**

¼ **teaspoon fine sea salt**

¼ **cup unsweetened cocoa powder, sifted**

½ **cup granulated sugar**

4 **large egg yolks**

¼ **cup packed light brown sugar**

4 **ounces semisweet chocolate, chopped**

¾ **cup stout beer**

Prepare an ice bath by filling a large bowl with ice cubes and 1 to 2 cups of water. Place a medium bowl fitted with a fine strainer inside the ice bath.

In a medium saucepan, combine the milk, cream, vanilla, salt, cocoa, and granulated sugar. Set over medium heat, stirring occasionally, until the mixture is warm and begins to steam, about 5 minutes.

In a medium bowl, whisk together the egg yolks and the brown sugar until well combined. Carefully whisk half of the warm milk mixture into the egg yolks, one ladleful at a time, until the egg mixture is warmed. Whisk the egg-milk mixture back into the saucepan. Cook the mixture over medium heat, stirring constantly with a wooden spoon, until the mixture is thick enough to coat the back of the spoon and registers around 175°F on an instant-read thermometer, about 5 to 7 minutes. Be careful not to boil the mixture.

Immediately strain the mixture through the fine strainer into the prepared ice bath. Stir in the chocolate until melted and smooth. Add the stout, stirring to combine. Cool the custard in the ice bath until it reaches room temperature, stirring often. Press plastic wrap against the surface of the custard and refrigerate until chilled, about 4 hours or up to 1 day.

Pour the chilled mixture into an ice cream maker. Freeze according to the manufacturer's directions. Transfer the ice cream to an airtight container, press plastic wrap against the ice cream surface, and freeze until it is firm and the flavor is ripened, at least 4 hours.

## CHOCOLATE STOUT WHOOPIE PIES

**MAKES ABOUT 20 WHOOPIE PIE HALVES**

**2 cups all-purpose flour**
**$^1/_4$ cup unsweetened cocoa powder**
**1 teaspoon baking powder**
**$^1/_2$ teaspoon baking soda**
**$^1/_4$ teaspoon fine sea salt**
**4 ounces (1 stick) unsalted butter, at room temperature**
**$^1/_2$ cup packed light brown sugar**
**$^1/_3$ cup granulated sugar**
**1 large egg**
**1 teaspoon vanilla extract**
**$^3/_4$ cup stout beer, divided**

In a medium bowl, sift together the flour, cocoa powder, baking powder, baking soda, and salt.

In a large bowl, beat the butter and sugars on medium-high speed until smooth, about 1 to 2 minutes. Add the egg and vanilla and beat until

combined. On low speed, add half of the stout. Add half of the flour mixture, beating until combined. Add the remaining stout, then the remaining flour mixture and beat until combined. Cover the dough with plastic wrap and chill in the refrigerator for 30 minutes, or until firm.

Preheat the oven to 350°F. Line baking sheets with parchment paper.

Using a spoon or spring-loaded scoop, drop the batter into 1$^1/_2$-tablespoon rounds onto prepared baking sheets, spacing 2 inches apart. Bake for about 10 minutes, or until the edges are set and the tops spring back when touched. Let cool on baking sheets before removing to wire racks to cool completely. Freeze the whoopie pie halves until frozen, at least 1 hour. Whoopie pie halves can be stored in airtight containers in the freezer for up to 1 month.

### For Decorating:
**Crushed pretzels (about $^1/_2$ cup), for rolling**

**TO ASSEMBLE,** place the crushed pretzels in a shallow dish. Top one whoopie pie half with a scoop of ice cream. Place another half on top and gently press down to form a sandwich. Roll the edges in the crushed pretzels. Immediately place the sandwich in the freezer. Repeat for the remaining whoopie pies. Freeze for at least 2 hours before serving.

# Margarita Ice Cream Sandwich

*A Margarita Ice Cream Sandwich may be better than an actual margarita. The Lime Ice Cream is refreshingly cool and tart with just enough sweetness. Then there are the Salted Tequila Cookies, which I know probably sound weird. Tequila, in a cookie? Just trust me: The cookies are beautifully soft, sweet, and salty with a little kick from the tequila. They're a favorite in my house.*

## LIME ICE CREAM

### MAKES ABOUT 1 QUART

**1¹/₂ cups whole milk**

**1¹/₂ cups heavy cream**

**¹/₂ teaspoon vanilla extract**

**³/₄ cup granulated sugar**

**¹/₄ teaspoon fine sea salt**

**4 large egg yolks**

**3 teaspoons lime zest
(from about 2 medium limes)**

**¹/₄ cup fresh lime juice
(from about 2 medium limes)**

**1 tablespoon tequila**

Prepare an ice bath by filling a large bowl with ice cubes and 1 to 2 cups of water. Place a medium bowl fitted with a fine strainer inside the ice bath.

In a medium saucepan, combine the milk, cream, vanilla, ¹/₂ cup sugar, and salt. Set over medium heat, stirring occasionally, until the mixture is warm and begins to steam, about 5 minutes.

In a medium bowl, whisk the remaining ¹/₄ cup sugar and the egg yolks until smooth and pale in color. Carefully whisk half of the warm milk mixture into the egg yolks, one ladleful at a time, until the egg mixture is warmed. Whisk the egg-milk mixture back into the saucepan. Cook the mixture over medium heat, stirring constantly with a wooden spoon, until the mixture is thick enough to coat the back of the spoon and registers around 175°F, about 5 to 7 minutes. Be careful not to boil the mixture.

Immediately strain the mixture through the fine strainer into the prepared ice bath. Cool the custard in the ice bath until it reaches room temperature, stirring often. Press plastic wrap against the custard and refrigerate until chilled, about 4 hours or up to 1 day.

Just before freezing, stir the lime zest and lime juice into the custard. Pour into an ice cream maker and freeze according to the manufacturer's directions. During the last minute of freezing, add the tequila. Transfer the ice cream to an airtight container, press plastic wrap against the ice cream, and freeze until it is firm and the flavor is ripened, at least 4 hours.

## SALTED TEQUILA COOKIES

**MAKES ABOUT 18 COOKIES**

**2 cups all-purpose flour**
**1 teaspoon baking soda**
**¼ teaspoon fine sea salt**
**4 ounces (1 stick) unsalted butter,
  at room temperature**
**¾ cup granulated sugar**
**¼ cup agave nectar**
**1 large egg**
**1 teaspoon vanilla extract**
**1 teaspoon orange zest**
**2 teaspoons tequila**
**Fine sea salt, for sprinkling**

Preheat the oven to 350°F. Line large baking sheets with parchment paper.

In a medium bowl, whisk the flour, baking soda, and salt to combine.

In a large bowl, use an electric mixer to beat the butter and sugar on medium speed until well combined and smooth, about 1 to 2 minutes. Add the agave nectar and egg and beat until combined. Add the vanilla extract, orange zest, and tequila and beat until combined. On low speed, slowly add the flour mixture and beat until combined.

Roll the dough into 2 tablespoon–sized balls. Place on prepared baking sheets and flatten with the bottom of a measuring cup to a 2-inch diameter. Sprinkle the dough rounds lightly with sea salt.

Bake for 10 to 12 minutes, or until the cookies are set and begin to brown. Let the cookies cool on the pans for 5 minutes, then remove to wire racks to cool completely. Freeze the cookies until frozen, at least 1 hour. Cookies can be stored in airtight containers in the freezer for up to 1 month.

**TO ASSEMBLE,** top one cookie with a scoop of ice cream. Place another cookie on top of the ice cream and gently press down to form a sandwich. Immediately place the sandwich in the freezer. Repeat for the remaining cookies. Freeze for at least 2 hours before serving.

# Sangria Ice Cream Sandwich

*In this perfect-for-summer sandwich, red wine is turned into ice cream and paired with super cit-rusy cookies for a treat you don't have to serve in a pitcher. You can use whatever red wine you prefer or have around. Make this recipe fruity and sweet by using a moscato rosa or more com-plex by using a full-bodied wine like cabernet.*

## RED WINE ICE CREAM

### MAKES ABOUT 1 QUART

- 1¼ cups whole milk
- 1¼ cups heavy cream
- 1 teaspoon vanilla extract
- ¾ cup granulated sugar
- Pinch of fine sea salt
- 5 large egg yolks
- ¾ cup red wine

Prepare an ice bath by filling a large bowl with ice cubes and 1 to 2 cups of water. Place a medium bowl fitted with a fine strainer inside the ice bath.

In a medium saucepan, combine the milk, cream, vanilla, ½ cup sugar, and salt. Set over medium heat, stirring occasionally, until the mixture is warm and begins to steam, about 5 minutes.

In a medium bowl, whisk together the egg yolks and the remaining ¼ cup sugar. Carefully whisk half of the warm milk mixture into the egg yolks, one ladleful at a time, until the egg mixture is warmed. Whisk the egg-milk mixture back into the saucepan. Cook the mixture over medium heat, stirring constantly with a wooden spoon, until the mixture is thick enough to coat the back of the spoon and registers around 175°F on an instant-read thermometer, about 5 to 7 minutes. Be careful not to boil the mixture.

Immediately strain the mixture through the fine strainer into the prepared ice bath. Add the wine, stirring to combine. Cool the custard in the ice bath until it reaches room temperature, stirring often. Press plastic wrap against the surface of the custard and refrigerate until chilled, about 4 hours or up to 1 day.

Pour the custard into an ice cream maker. Freeze according to the manufacturer's directions. Transfer the ice cream to an airtight container, press plastic wrap against the ice cream surface, and freeze until it is firm and the flavor is ripened, at least 4 hours.

# TRIPLE CITRUS COOKIES

**MAKES ABOUT 18 COOKIES**

2 cups all-purpose flour

$^1/_2$ teaspoon baking soda

$^1/_4$ teaspoon fine sea salt

5 ounces (1$^1/_4$ sticks) unsalted butter, at room temperature

$^3/_4$ cup granulated sugar

1 large egg

1 tablespoon milk

1 teaspoon vanilla extract

1 teaspoon grated lime zest

1 teaspoon grated lemon zest

1 teaspoon grated orange zest

Preheat the oven to 350°F. Line large baking sheets with parchment paper or silicone baking mats.

In a medium bowl, whisk together the flour, baking soda, and salt to combine.

In a large bowl, use an electric mixer to beat the butter and sugar on medium-high speed until well combined and smooth, about 1 to 2 minutes. Add the egg, milk, and vanilla and beat until combined. Beat in the lime zest, lemon zest, and orange zest. On low speed, slowly add the flour mixture and beat until combined.

Roll the dough into 2 tablespoon–sized balls. Place on prepared baking sheets and flatten with the bottom of a measuring cup to a 2-inch diameter.

Bake for 10 to 12 minutes, or until the cookies are set and begin to brown. Let the cookies cool on the pan for 5 minutes, then remove to a wire rack to cool completely. Freeze the cookies until frozen, at least 1 hour. Cookies can be stored in airtight containers in the freezer for up to 1 month.

**TO ASSEMBLE,** top one cookie with a scoop of ice cream. Place another cookie on top of the ice cream and gently press down to form a sandwich. Immediately place the sandwich in the freezer. Repeat for the remaining cookies. Freeze for at least 2 hours before serving.

# Tiramisu Ice Cream Sandwich

*The Italian word tiramisù means "pick me up," and with chocolate, rum, and espresso, this delightful treat is bound to do just that. It may seem strange to add rum to ice cream, but let me tell you, tiramisu is better than ever in the form of an ice cream sandwich.* Buon appetito!

## MASCARPONE CHOCOLATE CHUNK ICE CREAM

**MAKES ABOUT 1 QUART**

**8 ounces mascarpone**
**1 cup whole milk**
**1 cup heavy cream**
**¾ cup granulated sugar**
**¼ teaspoon fine sea salt**
**1 teaspoon vanilla extract**
**½ cup semisweet chocolate chunks**
**3 tablespoons dark rum**

In the bowl of a blender or food processor, puree the mascarpone, milk, cream, sugar, salt, and vanilla until smooth, scraping down the sides of the bowl as necessary. Transfer the mixture to a medium bowl and press plastic wrap against the surface. Refrigerate until completely chilled, at least 30 minutes.

Pour the chilled mixture into an ice cream maker. Freeze according to the manufacturer's directions. During the last 5 minutes of freezing, add the chocolate chunks and rum. Transfer the ice cream to an airtight container, press plastic wrap against the ice cream surface, and freeze until it is firm and the flavor is ripened, at least 4 hours.

## ESPRESSO COOKIES

**MAKES ABOUT 20 COOKIES**

**1¾ cups all-purpose flour**
**1 tablespoon instant espresso powder**
**½ teaspoon baking soda**
**¼ teaspoon fine sea salt**
**4 ounces (1 stick) unsalted butter, at room temperature**
**⅓ cup granulated sugar**
**½ cup packed light brown sugar**

**1 tablespoon milk**

**1 large egg**

**1 large egg yolk**

**2 teaspoons vanilla extract**

Preheat the oven to 350°F. Line baking sheets with parchment paper or silicone baking mats.

In a medium bowl, whisk together the flour, espresso powder, baking soda, and salt.

In a large bowl, use an electric mixer to beat the butter and sugars on medium-high speed until well combined and smooth, about 1 to 2 minutes. Add the milk, egg, egg yolk, and vanilla and beat until combined. On low speed, gradually add the flour mixture and beat until just combined.

Using a spoon or spring-loaded scoop, drop 2 tablespoon–sized balls of dough onto prepared baking sheets.

Bake for about 10 minutes, or until the edges are slightly browned. Let cool on baking sheets for 5 minutes before removing to wire racks to cool completely. Freeze the cookies until frozen, at least 1 hour. Cookies can be stored in airtight containers in the freezer for up to 1 month.

## For Decorating:

**Unsweetened cocoa powder (about 2 tablespoons), for dusting**

TO ASSEMBLE, top one cookie with a scoop of ice cream. Place another cookie on top of the ice cream and gently press down to form a sandwich. Immediately place the sandwich in the freezer. Repeat for the remaining cookies. Freeze for at least 2 hours. Dust lightly with cocoa powder before serving.

# Piña Colada Ice Cream Sandwich

*One bite of this island-inspired ice cream sandwich and you're transported to a warm beach with white sand and clear blue waters. It's the next best thing to a tropical vacation in paradise—no sunscreen necessary!*

## PINEAPPLE-RUM ICE CREAM

### MAKES ABOUT 1½ QUARTS

1½ **cups whole milk**

1½ **cups heavy cream**

1 **teaspoon vanilla extract**

¾ **cup granulated sugar, divided**

¼ **teaspoon fine sea salt**

4 **large egg yolks**

1 **(8-ounce) can crushed pineapple with juices**

3 **tablespoons light rum**

Prepare an ice bath by filling a large bowl with ice cubes and 1 to 2 cups of water. Place a medium bowl fitted with a fine strainer inside the ice bath.

In a medium saucepan, combine the milk, cream, vanilla, ½ cup sugar, and salt. Set over medium heat, stirring occasionally, until the mixture is warm and begins to steam, about 5 minutes.

In a medium bowl, whisk together the egg yolks and the remaining ¼ cup sugar. Carefully whisk half of the warm milk mixture into the egg yolks, one ladleful at a time, until the egg mixture is warmed. Whisk the egg-milk mixture back into the saucepan. Cook the mixture over medium heat, stirring constantly with a wooden spoon, until the mixture is thick enough to coat the back of the spoon and registers around 175°F on an instant-read thermometer, about 5 to 7 minutes. Be careful not to boil the mixture.

Immediately strain the mixture through the fine strainer into the prepared ice bath. Cool the custard in the ice bath until it reaches room temperature, stirring often. Press plastic wrap against the surface of the custard and refrigerate until chilled, about 4 hours or up to 1 day.

Pour the chilled mixture into an ice cream

maker. Freeze according to the manufacturer's directions. During the last 5 minutes of freezing, add the pineapple with juices and the rum. Transfer the ice cream to an airtight container, press plastic wrap against the ice cream surface, and freeze until it is firm and the flavor is ripened, at least 4 hours.

## COCONUT COOKIES

**MAKES ABOUT 20 COOKIES**

1½ **cups all-purpose flour**
½ **teaspoon baking soda**
¼ **teaspoon fine sea salt**
4 **ounces (1 stick) unsalted butter, at room temperature**
⅓ **cup granulated sugar**
⅓ **cup packed light brown sugar**
1 **large egg**
1 **large egg yolk**
¼ **teaspoon coconut extract**
1⅓ **cups sweetened shredded coconut**

Preheat the oven to 350°F. Line large baking sheets with parchment paper or silicone baking mats.

In a medium bowl, whisk together the flour, baking soda, and salt to combine.

In a large bowl, use an electric mixer to beat the butter and sugars on medium-high speed until well combined and smooth, about 1 to 2 minutes. Add the egg, egg yolk, and coconut extract and beat until combined. Add the shredded coconut and beat until combined. On low speed, slowly add the flour mixture and beat until combined.

Roll the dough into 2 tablespoon–sized balls. Place on prepared baking sheets and flatten with the palm of your hand.

Bake for 10 minutes, or until the cookies are set and begin to brown, rotating sheets halfway through. Let the cookies cool on the pan for 5 minutes, then remove to wire racks to cool completely. Freeze the cookies until frozen, at least 1 hour. Cookies can be stored in airtight containers in the freezer for up to 1 month.

**TO ASSEMBLE,** top one cookie with a scoop of ice cream. Place another cookie on top of the ice cream and gently press down to form a sandwich. Immediately place the sandwich in the freezer. Repeat for remaining cookies. Freeze for at least 2 hours before serving.

*Tip:* If you don't have coconut extract for the cookies, just use vanilla extract.

# Mint Julep Ice Cream Sandwich

*Anytime you add bourbon to a dessert, you're bound to pique some interest—and for good reason. Bourbon takes any dessert to the next level, inviting your mouth to savor every bite. So the next time you put on a big frilly Kentucky Derby hat and bet on a horse, remember to make a batch of these ice cream sandwiches to really celebrate.*

## FRESH MINT BOURBON ICE CREAM

### MAKES ABOUT 1 QUART

1¹⁄₂ **cups whole milk**
1¹⁄₂ **cups heavy cream**
**2 cups lightly packed fresh mint leaves**
³⁄₄ **cup granulated sugar, divided**
¹⁄₄ **teaspoon fine sea salt**
**4 large egg yolks**
**3 tablespoons bourbon**

In a medium saucepan, combine the milk, cream, mint, ¹⁄₂ cup sugar, and salt. Set over medium-high heat until the mixture is hot but not boiling, and the sugar is dissolved. Remove from heat, cover, and let the mint steep for 30 minutes.

Strain the mixture, pressing on the mint leaves to extract flavor, and then return the mixture to the saucepan. Discard the mint leaves. Set the mixture over medium-high heat and cook for about 5 minutes, or until warm again.

Prepare an ice bath by filling a large bowl with ice cubes and 1 to 2 cups of water. Place a medium bowl fitted with a fine strainer inside the ice bath.

In a medium bowl, whisk together the egg yolks and the remaining ¹⁄₄ cup sugar. Carefully whisk half of the warm milk mixture into the egg yolks, one ladleful at a time, until the egg mixture is warmed. Whisk the egg-milk mixture back into the saucepan. Cook the mixture over medium heat, stirring constantly with a wooden spoon, until the mixture is thick enough to coat the back of the spoon and registers around 175°F on an instant-read thermometer, about 5 to 7 minutes. Be careful not to boil the mixture.

Immediately strain the mixture through the fine strainer into the prepared ice bath. Cool the custard in the ice bath until it reaches room temperature, stirring often. Press plastic wrap against the the custard and refrigerate until chilled, about 4 hours or up to 1 day.

Pour the chilled mixture into an ice cream maker. Freeze according to the manufacturer's directions. During the last 2 minutes of freezing, add the bourbon.

If using a decorative cookie cutter, line a large rimmed baking sheet with parchment paper or plastic wrap. Spread freshly churned ice cream evenly over lined baking sheet. Press additional plastic wrap against the ice cream. Freeze until firm, at least 2 hours or up to 3 days. Alternatively, transfer the ice cream to an airtight container, press plastic wrap against the ice cream, and freeze until it is firm, at least 4 hours.

## BOURBON SHORTBREAD COOKIES

**MAKES ABOUT 28 COOKIES**

**2 cups all-purpose flour**

**¼ teaspoon fine sea salt**

**8 ounces (2 sticks) unsalted butter, at room temperature**

**¾ cup confectioners' sugar**

**3 tablespoons bourbon**

In a medium bowl, whisk together the flour and salt.

In a large bowl, use an electric mixer on medium-high speed to beat the butter until smooth. Add the sugar and beat until well combined. Beat in the bourbon. On low speed, slowly add the flour mixture and beat until combined. Flatten the dough into a disk and wrap in plastic. Chill for at least 1 hour, or until firm.

Preheat the oven to 350°F. Line large baking sheets with parchment paper or silicone baking mats.

Place the dough between two large pieces of parchment paper or plastic wrap. Roll the dough out into a ¼-inch thickness. Use a 2½-inch round cookie cutter to cut circles from the dough. Place dough rounds on prepared baking sheets and bake for about 10 minutes, or until the cookies are set and lightly browned. Cool on the pans for 5 minutes before removing the cookies to wire racks to cool completely. Freeze the cookies until frozen, at least 1 hour. Cookies can be stored in airtight containers in the freezer for up to 1 month.

**TO ASSEMBLE,** if using a decorative cookie cutter, remove the ice cream sheet from the freezer. Using the same cookie cutter, cut out a round of ice cream and sandwich it between two cookies. Repeat for the remaining cookies, working quickly. If the ice cream begins to melt, return to the freezer until firm again. Freeze the sandwiches until firm, at least 1 hour. Alternatively, top one cookie with a scoop of ice cream. Place another cookie on top of the ice cream and gently press down to form a sandwich. Immediately place the sandwich in the freezer. Repeat for the remaining cookies. Freeze for at least 2 hours before serving.

# Mudslide Ice Cream Sandwich

*Also known as Pure Bliss, this ice cream sandwich is full of dessert decadence. The ice cream is ridiculously smooth and rich with swirls of thick chocolate fudge sauce. Not to mention, the cookies have a hefty dose of coffee liqueur. If you have any ice cream or cookies left by the time you're ready to assemble the sandwiches, you're in for a scrumptious treat worthy of any occasion.*

## IRISH CREAM ICE CREAM

### MAKES ABOUT 1¹/₂ QUARTS

1¹/₂ cups whole milk
1¹/₂ cups heavy cream
1 teaspoon vanilla extract
³/₄ cup granulated sugar, divided
¹/₄ teaspoon salt
4 large egg yolks
¹/₄ cup Irish cream liqueur (such as Bailey's)
Fudge Swirl (page 50)

Prepare an ice bath by filling a large bowl with ice cubes and 1 to 2 cups of water. Place a medium bowl fitted with a fine strainer inside the ice bath.

In a medium saucepan, combine the milk, cream, vanilla, ¹/₂ cup sugar, and salt. Set over medium heat, stirring occasionally, until the mixture is warm and begins to steam, about 5 minutes.

In a medium bowl, whisk together the egg yolks and the remaining ¹/₄ cup sugar. Carefully whisk half of the warm milk mixture into the egg yolks, one ladleful at a time, until the egg mixture is warmed. Whisk the egg-milk mixture back into the saucepan. Cook the mixture over medium heat, stirring constantly, until the mixture is thick enough to coat the back of the spoon and registers around 175°F on an instant-read thermometer, about 5 to 7 minutes. Be careful not to boil the mixture.

Immediately strain the mixture through the fine strainer into the prepared ice bath. Cool the custard in the ice bath until it reaches room temperature, stirring often. Press plastic wrap against the surface of the custard and refrigerate until chilled, about 4 hours or up to 1 day.

While the custard is chilling, make the Fudge Swirl (page 50). Keep at room temperature and set aside until ready to use. If making beforehand, Fudge Swirl can be stored in the fridge for up to 2 days, but should be brought to room temperature before it's added to the ice cream so that it's easier to pour.

Pour the chilled mixture into an ice cream maker. Freeze according to the manufacturer's directions. During the last minutes of freezing, add the Irish cream. Transfer the ice cream to an airtight container in batches, spooning the Fudge Swirl in between layers of ice cream in a swirled pattern. Press plastic wrap against the ice cream, and freeze until it is firm, at least 4 hours.

## MOCHA COOKIES

**MAKES ABOUT 20 COOKIES**

1³/₄ **cups all-purpose flour**
¹/₄ **cup unsweetened cocoa powder**
2 **tablespoons instant espresso powder**
1 **teaspoon baking soda**
1 **teaspoon baking powder**
¹/₄ **teaspoon salt**
4 **ounces (1 stick) unsalted butter, at room temperature**
¹/₂ **cup granulated sugar**
¹/₂ **cup packed light brown sugar**
1 **large egg**
1 **teaspoon vanilla extract**
¹/₄ **cup coffee liqueur (such as Kahlua)**

Preheat the oven to 350°F. Line baking sheets with parchment paper or silicone baking mats.

In a medium bowl, sift together the flour, cocoa powder, espresso powder, baking soda, baking powder, and salt.

In a large bowl, use an electric mixer to beat the butter and sugars on medium-high speed until well combined and smooth, 1 to 2 minutes. Add the egg and vanilla and beat until combined. Add the coffee liqueur. On low speed, gradually add the flour mixture and beat until combined.

Using a spoon or spring-loaded scoop, drop 2 tablespoon–sized balls of dough onto prepared baking sheets. Flatten rounds with the palm of your hand.

Bake for about 10 minutes, or until the cookies are set. Let cool on baking sheets for 5 minutes before removing to wire racks to cool completely. Freeze the cookies until frozen, at least 1 hour. Cookies can be stored in airtight containers in the freezer for up to 1 month.

**TO ASSEMBLE,** top one cookie with a scoop of ice cream. Place another cookie on top of the ice cream and gently press down to form a sandwich. Immediately place the sandwich in the freezer. Repeat for remaining cookies. Freeze for at least 2 hours before serving.

# Holiday

WHO SAYS YOU CAN'T HAVE ICE CREAM WHEN IT'S CHILLY OUTSIDE? Why must we miss out on one of the world's greatest treats just because sleigh bells are ringing and snow is glistening? There's a reason that holiday-inspired frozen treats and drinks are so popular in stores and shops. People love frozen treats all the time, anytime. With flavors like Apple Pie, Pumpkin Pie, Hot Cocoa, and Eggnog, what's not to love about this chapter?

I had so much fun thinking up these recipes, it was hard to choose which flavors to include. There's even Candy Corn Ice Cream, which even the staunchest candy corn-hater will secretly enjoy. So whether you're whipping up a batch of these festive sandwiches for a holiday party or in the middle of summer, you're bound to feel spirited and joyful.

# Halloween Ice Scream Sandwich

### ● ● ● ● ● ● ● ● ● ● ● MAKES ABOUT 12 ICE CREAM SANDWICHES ● ● ● ● ● ● ● ● ● ●

*What could be more fun than Candy Corn Ice Cream and Monster Cookies to celebrate Halloween? Candy Corn Ice Cream is a bright, yellowy-orange color that will please both kids and adults. Trust me: Even those who don't particularly like candy corn will like this ice cream. If you've never had thick and chewy Monster Cookies, they're filled with peanut butter, oats, chocolate, and candy. They're definitely more scrumptious than spooky!*

## CANDY CORN ICE CREAM

**MAKES ABOUT 1 QUART**

**1½ cups whole milk**
**1½ cups heavy cream**
**1 (11-ounce) bag candy corn**
**¼ teaspoon fine sea salt**
**3 large egg yolks**

Prepare an ice bath by filling a large bowl with ice cubes and 1 to 2 cups of water. Place a medium bowl fitted with a fine strainer inside the ice bath.

In a medium saucepan, combine the milk, cream, candy corn, and salt. Set over medium heat, stirring occasionally, until the candy corn begins to dissolve and the mixture turns an orange color, about 5 minutes.

In a medium bowl, whisk the egg yolks until smooth. Carefully whisk half of the warm milk mixture into the egg yolks, one ladleful at a time, until the egg mixture is warmed. Whisk the egg-milk mixture back into the saucepan. Cook the mixture over medium heat, stirring constantly with a wooden spoon, until the mixture is thick enough to coat the back of the spoon and registers around 175°F on an instant-read thermometer, about 5 to 7 minutes. Be careful not to boil the mixture.

Immediately pour the mixture through the strainer into the prepared ice bath. Discard any remaining candy corn pieces. Cool the custard in the ice bath until it reaches room temperature, stirring often. Press plastic wrap against the surface of the custard and refrigerate until chilled, about 4 hours or up to 1 day.

Pour the chilled mixture into an ice cream maker. Freeze according to the manufacturer's directions. Transfer the ice cream to an airtight container, press plastic wrap against the ice cream surface, and freeze until it is firm and the flavor is ripened, at least 4 hours.

## MONSTER COOKIES

**MAKES ABOUT 24 COOKIES**

**2 ounces (4 tablespoons) unsalted butter, at room temperature**

**³/₄ cup peanut butter**

**¹/₂ cup granulated sugar**

**¹/₂ cup packed light brown sugar**

**1 large egg**

**1 large egg yolk**

**1 teaspoon vanilla extract**

**2 cups rolled oats**

**1 teaspoon baking soda**

**¹/₄ teaspoon salt**

**¹/₂ cup semisweet chocolate chips**

**1 cup M&M candies**

Preheat the oven to 350°F. Line baking sheets with parchment paper or silicone baking mats.

In a large bowl, use an electric mixer to beat the butter, peanut butter, and sugars on medium-high speed until well combined and smooth, about 1 to 2 minutes. Beat in the egg, egg yolk, and vanilla. Add the oats, baking soda, and salt and beat until combined. Fold in the chocolate chips and M&M candies with a rubber spatula.

Using a spoon or spring-loaded scoop, drop 2 tablespoon–sized balls of dough onto prepared baking sheets. Flatten slightly with the bottom of a measuring cup.

Bake for about 10 minutes, or until the edges are slightly browned. Let cool on baking sheets for 5 minutes before removing to wire racks to cool completely. Freeze the cookies until frozen, at least 1 hour. Cookies can be stored in airtight containers in the freezer for up to 1 month.

**TO ASSEMBLE,** top one cookie with a scoop of ice cream. Place another cookie on top of the ice cream and gently press down to form a sandwich. Repeat for the remaining cookies. Freeze for at least 1¹/₂ hours before serving.

*Tip:* Use your favorite Halloween candy in place of the M&Ms in the cookies, such as chopped chocolate bars like Hershey's, Snickers, 3 Musketeers, Rolos, Twix, or whatever else is left over from trick-or-treating.

# Maple-Nut Ice Cream Sandwich

*I'm a firm believer that texture has as much to do with enjoying food as taste does. This sandwich feels as good as it tastes. It's chewy, crunchy, soft, and smooth with that distinct maple sweetness and a bit of nuttiness. Be sure to use real maple syrup—none of that artificial stuff you drench your pancakes in—because it is the key flavor component in the ice cream. In fact, there's no sugar at all in the ice cream, only maple syrup!*

## MAPLE ICE CREAM

### MAKES ABOUT 1 QUART

1½ **cups whole milk**

1½ **cups heavy cream**

¼ **teaspoon fine sea salt**

1 **teaspoon vanilla extract**

5 **large egg yolks**

¾ **cup pure maple syrup (preferably Grade B)**

Prepare an ice bath by filling a large bowl with ice cubes and 1 to 2 cups of water. Place a medium bowl fitted with a fine strainer inside the ice bath.

In a medium saucepan, combine the milk, cream, salt, and vanilla. Set over medium heat, stirring occasionally, until the mixture is warm and begins to steam, about 5 minutes.

In a medium bowl, whisk the egg yolks until smooth and light in color. Carefully whisk half of the warm milk mixture into the egg yolks, one ladleful at a time, until the egg mixture is warmed. Whisk the egg-milk mixture back into the saucepan. Cook the mixture over medium heat, stirring constantly with a wooden spoon, until the mixture is thick enough to coat the back of the spoon and registers around 175°F on an instant-read thermometer, about 5 to 7 minutes. Be careful not to boil the mixture.

Immediately strain the mixture through the fine strainer into the prepared ice bath. Stir in the maple syrup. Cool the custard in the ice bath until it reaches room temperature, stirring often. Press plastic wrap against the surface of the custard and refrigerate until chilled, about 4 hours or up to 1 day.

Pour the chilled mixture into an ice cream maker. Freeze according to the manufacturer's directions. Transfer the ice cream to an airtight container, press plastic wrap against the ice cream surface, and freeze until it is firm and the flavor is ripened, at least 2 hours.

# WHITE CHOCOLATE – PECAN BLONDIES

## MAKES ABOUT 32 BLONDIES

$1\frac{1}{2}$ **cups all-purpose flour**
$\frac{1}{4}$ **teaspoon baking soda**
$\frac{1}{4}$ **teaspoon fine sea salt**
**8 ounces (2 sticks) unsalted butter, melted**
**2 cups packed light brown sugar**
**2 large eggs**
**1 teaspoon vanilla extract**
$\frac{1}{2}$ **cup white chocolate chips**
$\frac{1}{2}$ **cup pecans, chopped**

Preheat the oven to 325°F. Spray two 8 x 8–inch baking pans with nonstick cooking spray. Line baking pans with parchment paper or foil, leaving an overhang, and spray with more nonstick cooking spray.

In a medium bowl, whisk together the flour, baking soda, and salt.

In a large bowl, stir the butter and sugar together until smooth. Add the eggs, one at a time, stirring after each addition, until completely combined. Add in the vanilla. Gradually add the flour mixture, stirring with a rubber spatula to combine. Fold in the chocolate chips and pecans.

Divide the batter evenly between the prepared pans. Bake until a toothpick inserted into the center of the blondies comes out with just a few moist crumbs attached, about 20 minutes. Do not over-bake. Let the blondies cool completely in pans on wire racks. Freeze the blondies in the pans until solid, about 4 hours or up to 3 days.

**TO ASSEMBLE,** allow the ice cream to sit at room temperature until softened, about 15 to 30 minutes. Pour about $2\frac{1}{2}$ cups of softened ice cream over one blondie sheet in the pan (you will have leftover ice cream). Using the parchment paper or foil, remove the remaining blondie sheet from its pan. Carefully and gently place the blondie sheet on top of the ice cream layer. Cover with plastic wrap and freeze until firm, at least 4 hours or overnight.

Remove from the freezer for 5 minutes, then cut into 16 squares. Serve immediately or wrap each square in plastic and return to the freezer for up to 1 week. If serving from the freezer, allow the sandwiches to sit at room temperature for 5 to 10 minutes before serving.

# Gingerbread Ice Cream Sandwich

*Fun and festive, these sandwiches are full of sugar and spice and everything nice. Not to mention, these Gingerbread Cookies are ultra soft and chewy, even after living in the freezer for days. This sandwich combines two of my favorite holiday foods, pumpkin from Thanksgiving and ginger-bread from Christmas. You'll be waiting all year for an excuse to make these sandwiches.*

## PUMPKIN SPICE ICE CREAM

### MAKES ABOUT 1½ QUARTS

- **1½ cups whole milk**
- **1½ cups heavy cream**
- **¾ cup packed light brown sugar, divided**
- **¼ teaspoon fine sea salt**
- **1 teaspoon vanilla extract**
- **4 large egg yolks**
- **1 teaspoon ground cinnamon**
- **¼ teaspoon ground ginger**
- **¼ teaspoon ground nutmeg**
- **1 cup fresh or unsweetened canned pumpkin puree**
- **1 tablespoon bourbon (optional)**

Prepare an ice bath by filling a large bowl with ice cubes and 1 to 2 cups of water. Place a medium bowl fitted with a fine strainer inside the ice bath.

In a medium saucepan, combine the milk, cream, ½ cup sugar, salt, and vanilla. Set over medium heat, stirring occasionally, until the mixture is warm and begins to steam, about 5 minutes.

In a medium bowl, whisk together the remaining ¼ cup sugar, egg yolks, cinnamon, ginger, and nutmeg until smooth. Carefully whisk half of the warm milk mixture into the egg yolks, one ladleful at a time, until the egg mixture is warmed. Whisk the egg-milk mixture back into the saucepan. Cook the mixture over medium heat, stirring constantly with a wooden spoon, until the mixture is thick enough to coat the back of the spoon and registers around 175°F on an instant-read thermometer, about 5 to 7 minutes. Be careful not to boil the mixture.

Immediately strain the mixture through the fine strainer into the prepared ice bath. Strain the pumpkin puree into the bowl and whisk to combine. Cool the custard in the ice bath until it reaches room temperature, stirring often. Press plastic wrap against the surface of the custard and refrigerate until chilled, about 4 hours or up to 1 day.

Pour the chilled mixture into an ice cream maker. Freeze according to the manufacturer's directions. During the last minutes of freezing, add the bourbon to the mixture, if using. Line a large rimmed baking sheet (or 2 smaller baking sheets if your freezer is small) with parchment paper. Spread the freshly churned ice cream evenly over the lined baking sheet. Press plastic wrap against the surface of the ice cream. Freeze until firm, at least 2 hours or up to 3 days.

## GINGERBREAD COOKIES

**MAKES ABOUT 24 GINGERBREAD MEN COOKIES**

**3 cups all-purpose flour**
**1 teaspoon baking powder**
**$^1/_2$ teaspoon baking soda**
**$^1/_2$ teaspoon fine sea salt**
**1$^1/_4$ teaspoons ground ginger**
**1 teaspoon ground cinnamon**
**$^1/_4$ teaspoon ground cloves**

**$^1/_4$ teaspoon ground nutmeg**
**6 ounces (1$^1/_2$ sticks) unsalted butter, at room temperature**
**$^1/_2$ cup packed light brown sugar**
**1 large egg**
**$^1/_2$ cup unsulfured molasses**

In a medium bowl, whisk together the flour, baking powder, baking soda, salt, ginger, cinnamon, cloves, and nutmeg to combine.

In a large bowl, use an electric mixer to beat the butter and sugar on medium-high speed until well combined and smooth, about 1 to 2 minutes. Add the egg and molasses and beat until combined. On low speed, slowly add the flour mixture and beat until combined. Shape the dough into a thick disk and wrap in plastic. Refrigerate until chilled, about 2 hours or up to 2 days.

Preheat the oven to 350°F. Line large baking sheets with parchment paper or silicone baking mats.

Remove the dough from the refrigerator and let stand for 5 to 10 minutes, or until warm enough to roll with ease. Place the chilled dough in between two large pieces of parchment paper or plastic wrap on a work surface. Roll the dough to a $^1/_4$-inch thickness. Use a gingerbread man cookie cutter to cut out shapes from the dough and place on prepared baking sheets, spreading at least a $\frac{1}{2}$ inch apart. Reroll remaining scraps of dough into $\frac{1}{4}$-inch thickness and cut out more shapes.

Bake for 10 to 12 minutes, or until the cookies are set and begin to brown slightly at the edges, rotating sheets halfway through. Let the cookies cool on the pans for 3 minutes, then remove to wire racks to cool completely.

Freeze the cookies until frozen, at least 1 hour. Cookies can be stored in airtight containers in the freezer for up to 1 month.

**TO ASSEMBLE,** remove the ice cream sheet from the freezer. Using the same gingerbread man cookie cutter, cut out a slice of ice cream and sandwich it between two cookies. Wrap the sandwich with plastic and freeze. Repeat for the remaining cookies, working quickly. If the ice cream begins to melt, return to the freezer until firm again. Freeze until firm, for at least 1 hour or up to 1 week. Let sit at room temperature for 5 to 10 minutes before serving.

*Tip:* Use a tall metal gingerbread man cookie cutter that is on the smaller side so it is easier to cut the ice cream without the cookie cutter getting stuck.

# Apple Pie Ice Cream Sandwich

*One bite of this sandwich and you'll be wishing there were a holiday every day. If you like a scoop of ice cream on top of your apple pie, then you'll fall in love with this Apple-Cinnamon Ice Cream. If you like big, chewy, and flavorful cookies, then you'll fall even harder for this holiday sandwich.*

## APPLE-CINNAMON ICE CREAM

**MAKES ABOUT 1½ QUARTS**

**1½ cups whole milk**

**1½ cups heavy cream**

**⅓ cup granulated sugar**

**1 teaspoon vanilla extract**

**4 large egg yolks**

**2 tablespoons unsalted butter**

**3 medium Granny Smith apples,
cored, peeled, and chopped
into small pieces**

**⅓ cup packed light brown sugar**

**¼ teaspoon fine sea salt**

**1 teaspoon ground cinnamon**

**¼ teaspoon ground nutmeg**

Prepare an ice bath by filling a large bowl with ice cubes and 1 to 2 cups of water. Place a medium bowl fitted with a fine strainer inside the ice bath.

In a medium saucepan, combine the milk, cream, granulated sugar, and vanilla. Set over medium heat, stirring occasionally, until the mixture is warm and begins to steam, about 5 minutes.

In a medium bowl, whisk the egg yolks until smooth and light in color. Carefully whisk half of the warm milk mixture into the egg yolks, one ladleful at a time, until the egg mixture is warmed. Whisk the egg-milk mixture back into the saucepan. Cook the mixture over medium heat, stirring constantly, until the mixture is thick enough to coat the back of the spoon and registers around 175°F, about 5 to 7 minutes. Be careful not to boil the mixture.

Immediately strain the mixture through the fine strainer into the prepared ice bath. Cool the custard in the ice bath, stirring often. Press plastic wrap against the custard and refrigerate until chilled, about 4 hours or up to 1 day.

While the custard is chilling, melt the butter in a medium saucepan set over medium heat.

Add the apples, brown sugar, salt, cinnamon, and nutmeg. Cook, stirring often, until the apples are tender. Let the mixture cool before placing it in an airtight container in the refrigerator to chill, about 4 hours or up to 1 day.

Pour the chilled custard into an ice cream maker. Freeze according to the manufacturer's directions. During the last minutes of freezing, add the chilled apple mixture. Transfer the ice cream to a storage container and press plastic wrap against the surface. Freeze until firm, at least 2 hours or up to 3 days.

## MOLASSES COOKIES

**MAKES ABOUT 22 COOKIES**

1½ **cups all-purpose flour**
2 **teaspoons baking soda**
½ **teaspoon fine sea salt**
½ **teaspoon ground ginger**
1 **teaspoon ground cinnamon**
½ **teaspoon ground cloves**
6 **ounces (1½ sticks) unsalted butter, at room temperature**
½ **cup granulated sugar, divided**
½ **cup light brown sugar**
½ **cup unsulfured molasses**
1 **large egg**

Preheat the oven to 325°F. Line large baking sheets with parchment paper.

In a medium bowl, whisk together the flour, baking soda, salt, ginger, cinnamon, and cloves to combine.

In a large bowl, beat the butter, ¼ cup granulated sugar, and brown sugar on medium-high speed until smooth, about 2 minutes. Add the molasses and egg and beat until combined. On low speed, slowly add the flour mixture and beat until combined.

Place the remaining ¼ cup granulated sugar in a shallow dish. Scoop 2-tablespoon rounds of dough. Roll each ball in the sugar and place on the prepared baking sheets, spacing 2 inches apart. Flatten the balls with the bottom of a measuring cup or glass.

Bake for 8 to 10 minutes, or until the cookies are golden and slightly puffed. Let cool completely. Freeze the cookies until frozen, at least 1 hour. Cookies can be stored in airtight containers in the freezer for up to 1 month.

### For Decorating:

**Sanding sugar (about ¼ cup), for rolling**

**TO ASSEMBLE,** top one cookie with a scoop of ice cream. Place another cookie on top and gently press down to form a sandwich. Roll the edges in the sanding sugar. Freeze for at least 1 hour before serving.

# Hot Cocoa Ice Cream Sandwich

*One sip of hot cocoa puts you in the mood for the holidays. But have you ever had frozen hot cocoa? This ice cream sandwich pays homage to that frozen treat, a treat that even Santa Claus himself will wish he had for his sleigh ride.*

## MARSHMALLOW ICE CREAM

### MAKES ABOUT 1 QUART

1½ **cups whole milk**
1½ **cups heavy cream**
⅓ **cup granulated sugar**
¼ **teaspoon fine sea salt**
2 **teaspoons vanilla extract**
5 **large egg yolks**
1 **cup marshmallow fluff**

Prepare an ice bath by filling a large bowl with ice cubes and 1 to 2 cups of water. Place a medium bowl fitted with a fine strainer inside the ice bath.

In a medium saucepan, combine the milk, cream, sugar, salt, and vanilla. Set over medium heat, stirring occasionally, until the mixture is warm and begins to steam, about 5 minutes.

In a medium bowl, whisk the egg yolks until smooth and light in color. Carefully whisk half of the warm milk mixture into the egg yolks, one ladleful at a time, until the egg mixture is warmed. Whisk the egg-milk mixture back into the saucepan. Cook the mixture over medium heat, stirring constantly with a wooden spoon, until the mixture is thick enough to coat the back of the spoon and registers around 175°F on an instant-read thermometer, about 5 to 7 minutes. Be careful not to boil the mixture.

Immediately strain the mixture through the fine strainer into the prepared ice bath. Cool the custard in the ice bath until it reaches room temperature, stirring often. Press plastic wrap against the surface of the custard and refrigerate until chilled, about 4 hours or up to 1 day.

Pour the chilled custard into an ice cream maker. Freeze according to the manufacturer's directions. In the last few minutes of freezing, add the marshmallow fluff, one spoonful at a time, until combined. Transfer the ice cream to an airtight container, press plastic wrap against the ice cream surface, and freeze until it is firm and the flavor is ripened, at least 2 hours.

## HOT COCOA COOKIES

**MAKES ABOUT 20 COOKIES**

1¼ **cups all-purpose flour**
⅓ **cup hot chocolate mix, powdered**
**1 teaspoon baking powder**
¼ **teaspoon fine sea salt**
**4 ounces (1 stick) unsalted butter,
   at room temperature**
¼ **cup granulated sugar**
½ **cup packed light brown sugar**
**1 large egg**
**1 large egg yolk**
½ **teaspoon vanilla extract**
**1 cup milk chocolate chips**

Preheat the oven to 350°F. Line baking sheets with parchment paper or silicone baking mats.

In a medium bowl, sift together the flour, hot chocolate mix, baking powder, and salt.

In a large bowl, use an electric mixer to beat the butter and sugars on medium-high speed until well combined and smooth, about 1 to 2 minutes. Add the egg and egg yolk and beat until combined. Beat in the vanilla extract. On low speed, gradually add the flour mixture and beat until combined. Fold in the chocolate chips with a rubber spatula. Chill for about 1 hour, or until the dough is no longer sticky.

Using a spoon or spring-loaded scoop, drop 2 tablespoon–sized balls of dough onto the prepared baking sheets.

Bake for about 10 minutes, or until the edges are set. Let cool on baking sheets for 5 minutes before removing to wire racks to cool completely. Freeze the cookies until frozen, at least 1 hour. Cookies can be stored in airtight containers in the freezer for up to 1 month.

**TO ASSEMBLE,** top one cookie with a scoop of ice cream. Place another cookie on top of the ice cream and gently press down to form a sandwich. Repeat for the remaining cookies. Freeze for at least 1 hour before serving.

# Candy Cane Ice Cream Sandwich

*Nothing says holiday more than the red and white swirl of a candy cane or peppermint candy. That's exactly what this ice cream sandwich looks like! Getting that beautiful swirl pattern on a cookie is easier than you might think. Plus, this Easy Vanilla Ice Cream recipe takes no time to whip up.*

## EASY VANILLA ICE CREAM

### MAKES ABOUT 1 QUART

1$\frac{1}{4}$ **cups whole milk**
$\frac{3}{4}$ **cup granulated sugar**
**2 cups heavy cream**
**1 tablespoon vanilla extract**
$\frac{1}{4}$ **teaspoon fine sea salt**

In a large bowl, use an electric mixer to beat the milk and sugar until the sugar is dissolved, about 1 to 2 minutes. Stir in the cream, vanilla, and salt until combined. If the mixture isn't cold, place in the refrigerator until chilled, about 30 minutes.

Pour the chilled mixture into an ice cream maker. Freeze according to the manufacturer's directions. Transfer the ice cream to an airtight container, press plastic wrap against the ice cream surface, and freeze until it is firm and the flavor is ripened, at least 2 hours.

## PEPPERMINT PINWHEEL COOKIES

### MAKES ABOUT 20 COOKIES

2$\frac{1}{4}$ **cups all-purpose flour**
$\frac{1}{2}$ **teaspoon baking powder**
$\frac{1}{4}$ **teaspoon fine sea salt**
**8 ounces (2 sticks) unsalted butter,
    at room temperature**
$\frac{3}{4}$ **cup granulated sugar**
**1 large egg**
$\frac{1}{2}$ **teaspoon vanilla extract**
**1 teaspoon peppermint extract**
$\frac{1}{2}$ **teaspoon red food coloring**

In a medium bowl, whisk together the flour, baking powder, and salt.

In a large bowl, use an electric mixer to beat the butter and sugar on medium-high speed until well combined and smooth, about 1 to 2 minutes. Add the egg and extracts and beat until combined. On low speed, gradually add

the flour mixture and beat until combined. Remove half of the dough from the bowl and set aside. Beat the food coloring into the remaining dough until evenly colored.

Place one portion of the dough in between two large sheets of parchment paper. Roll the dough out into a large rectangle about ¼-inch thick. Repeat with the second portion. Carefully place the red dough rectangle on top of the plain dough rectangle. Trim the edges if necessary. Using the parchment paper as a guide to prevent sticking, roll the long side of the dough into a tight log, creating a pinwheel effect. Wrap the log in plastic wrap and refrigerate for at least 2 hours or up to 2 days.

When ready to bake, preheat the oven to 350°F. Line large baking sheets with parchment paper or silicone baking mats.

Use a sharp knife to cut the dough log into ½-inch-thick slices. Place the slices on the prepared baking sheets, spacing 2 inches apart. Bake for 10 to 12 minutes, or until set.

Let cool for 2 minutes before removing the cookies to wire racks to cool completely. Freeze the cookies until frozen, at least 1 hour. Cookies can be stored in airtight containers in the freezer for up to 1 month.

## For Decorating:

**Crushed candy canes (about 6 candy canes), for rolling**

**TO ASSEMBLE,** place the crushed candy canes in a shallow dish. Top one cookie with a scoop of ice cream. Place another cookie on top of the ice cream and gently press down to form a sandwich. Roll the edges in the crushed candy canes and repeat for the remaining cookies. Freeze for at least 1 hour before serving.

*Tip:* The best way to crush candy canes is to place them in a resealable bag and pound them with a mallet or rolling pin until coarsely crushed.

# Eggnog Ice Cream Sandwich

*Even if you don't like eggnog, I know you won't be able to get enough of this Eggnog Ice Cream Sandwich. Eggnog is about a million times better in ice cream form! If you don't believe me, you're just going to have to make it and try for yourself.*

## EGGNOG ICE CREAM

### MAKES ABOUT 1 QUART

1¹/₂ **cups whole milk**
1¹/₂ **cups heavy cream**
³/₄ **cup granulated sugar, divided**
¹/₄ **teaspoon fine sea salt**
6 **large egg yolks**
1 **teaspoon vanilla extract**
³/₄ **teaspoon ground nutmeg**
2 **tablespoons dark rum or bourbon**

Prepare an ice bath by filling a large bowl with ice cubes and 1 to 2 cups of water. Place a medium bowl fitted with a fine strainer inside the ice bath.

In a medium saucepan, combine the milk, cream, ¹/₂ cup sugar, and salt. Set over medium heat, stirring occasionally, until the mixture is warm and begins to steam, about 5 minutes.

In a medium bowl, whisk together the remaining ¹/₄ cup sugar and egg yolks until smooth. Carefully whisk half of the warm milk mixture into the egg yolks, one ladleful at a time, until the egg mixture is warmed. Whisk the egg-milk mixture back into the saucepan. Cook the mixture over medium heat, stirring constantly with a wooden spoon, until the mixture is thick enough to coat the back of the spoon and registers around 175°F on an instant-read thermometer, about 5 to 7 minutes. Be careful not to boil the mixture.

Immediately strain the mixture through the fine strainer into the prepared ice bath. Add the vanilla and nutmeg, stirring to combine. Cool the custard in the ice bath until it reaches room temperature, stirring often. Press plastic wrap against the surface of the custard and refrigerate until chilled, about 4 hours or up to 1 day.

Pour the chilled custard into an ice cream maker. Freeze according to the manufacturer's directions. During the last minute of freezing, add the alcohol. Transfer the ice cream to an airtight container, press plastic wrap against the ice cream surface, and freeze until it is firm and the flavor is ripened, at least 2 hours.

# BROWN SUGAR COOKIES

**MAKES ABOUT 20 COOKIES**

1³/₄ **cups all-purpose flour**
½ **teaspoon baking powder**
¼ **teaspoon baking soda**
¼ **teaspoon fine sea salt**
¼ **teaspoon ground nutmeg**
¼ **teaspoon ground ginger**
½ **teaspoon ground cinnamon**
4 **ounces (1 stick) unsalted butter, at room temperature**
2 **ounces cream cheese, at room temperature**
1 **cup packed light brown sugar**
1 **large egg**
1 **teaspoon vanilla extract**

Preheat the oven to 350°F. Line large baking sheets with parchment paper or silicone baking mats.

In a medium bowl, whisk together the flour, baking powder, baking soda, salt, nutmeg, ginger, and cinnamon to combine.

In a large bowl, use an electric mixer to beat the butter, cream cheese, and sugar on medium-high speed until well combined and smooth, about 1 to 2 minutes. Add the egg and vanilla and beat until combined. On low speed, slowly add the flour mixture and beat until combined.

Roll dough into 2 tablespoon–sized balls. Place on prepared baking sheets and flatten with the bottom of a measuring cup to a 2-inch diameter.

Bake for 10 to 12 minutes, or until the cookies are set and begin to brown, rotating sheets halfway through. Let the cookies cool on the pans for 5 minutes, then remove to wire racks to cool completely. Freeze the cookies until frozen, at least 1 hour. Cookies can be stored in airtight containers in the freezer for up to 1 month.

**TO ASSEMBLE,** top one cookie with a scoop of ice cream. Place another cookie on top of the ice cream and gently press down to form a sandwich. Repeat with the remaining cookies. Freeze for at least 1 hour before serving.

# Formulas for Metric Conversions

**Ounces to grams**   multiply ounces by 28.35
**Pounds to grams**   multiply pounds by 453.5
**Cups to liters**   multiply cups by .24
**Fahrenheit to Centigrade**   subtract 32 from Fahrenheit, multiply by 5 and divide by 9

## Metric Equivalents for Volume

| U.S. | Metric |
|---|---|
| $1/8$ tsp. | 0.6 ml |
| $1/4$ tsp. | 1.2 ml |
| $1/2$ tsp. | 2.5 ml |
| $3/4$ tsp. | 3.7 ml |
| 1 tsp. | 5 ml |
| $1 1/2$ tsp. | 7.4 ml |
| 2 tsp. | 10 ml |
| 1 Tbsp. | 15 ml |
| $1 1/2$ Tbsp. | 22.0 ml |
| 2 Tbsp. ($1/8$ cup/1 fl. oz) | 30 ml |
| 3 Tbsp. | 45 ml |
| $1/4$ cup (2 fl. oz) | 59 ml |
| $1/3$ cup | 79 ml |
| $1/2$ cup (4 fl. oz) | 118 ml |
| $2/3$ cup | 158 ml |
| $3/4$ cup (6 fl. oz) | 178 ml |
| 1 cup (8 fl. oz) | 237 ml |
| $1 1/4$ cups | 300 ml |
| $1 1/2$ cups | 355 ml |
| $1 3/4$ cups | 425 ml |
| 2 cups (1 pint/16 fl. oz) | 500 ml |
| 3 cups | 725 ml |
| 4 cups (1 quart/32 fl.oz) | .95 liters |
| 16 cups (1 gallon/128 fl.oz) | 3.8 liters |

## Oven Temperatures

| Degrees Fahrenheit | Degrees Centigrade | British Gas Marks |
|---|---|---|
| 200° | 93° | — |
| 250° | 120° | $1/2$ |
| 275° | 140° | 1 |
| 300° | 150° | 2 |
| 325° | 165° | 3 |
| 350° | 175° | 4 |
| 375° | 190° | 5 |
| 400° | 200° | 6 |
| 450° | 230° | 8 |

## Metric Equivalents for Weight

| U.S. | Metric |
|---|---|
| 1 oz | 28 g |
| 2 oz | 57 g |
| 3 oz | 85 g |
| 4 oz | 113 g |
| 5 oz | 142 g |
| 6 oz | 170 g |
| 7 oz | 198 g |
| 8 oz | 227 g |
| 16 oz (1 lb.) | 454 g |
| 2.2 lbs. | 1 kilogram |

## Metric Equivalents for Butter

| U.S. | Metric |
|---|---|
| 2 tsp. | 10 g |
| 1 Tbsp. | 15 g |
| $1 1/2$ Tbsp. | 22.5 g |
| 2 Tbsp. (1 oz) | 27 g |
| 3 Tbsp. | 42 g |
| 4 Tbsp. | 56 g |
| 4 oz. (1 stick) | 110 g |
| 8 oz. (2 sticks) | 220 g |

## Metric Equivalents for Length

| U.S. | Metric |
|---|---|
| $1/4$ inch | .65 cm |
| $1/2$ inch | 1.25 cm |
| 1 inch | 2.50 cm |
| 2 inches | 5.00 cm |
| 3 inches | 6.00 cm |
| 4 inches | 8.00 cm |
| 5 inches | 11.00 cm |
| 6 inches | 15.00 cm |
| 7 inches | 18.00 cm |
| 8 inches | 20.00 cm |
| 9 inches | 23.00 cm |
| 12 inches | 30.50 cm |
| 15 inches | 38.00 cm |

# Acknowledgments

THIS COOKBOOK WOULDN'T EXIST TODAY IF IT WEREN'T FOR THE LOVE and support from so many people I feel lucky to have in my life. My life hasn't been the same since Holly from Hollan Publishing told me she thought I had a cookbook in me. Thanks to Holly and Allan for guiding me through the publishing world. Another thanks to them for taking the beautiful photos that fill the pages of this book, despite photographing against all odds. Thanks to my editor, Jordana, and designer, Amanda, and everyone at Running Press for believing that the world needed a cookbook dedicated to ice cream sandwiches.

None of this would have happened if I hadn't decided to start a food blog one day in April of 2009. I'd like to thank every single person who has ever visited Handle the Heat, who has ever commented, e-mailed, Facebooked, or tweeted to me. Every time I hear that someone has tried and loved one of my recipes, I am filled with joy and am reminded of why I continue to spend so many hours in the kitchen. I'd also like to thank all my fellow food bloggers, who have always been there for me to offer their guidance, love, and support. I love all of you, even if we've never "met" in person! Another thanks goes to every teacher who has ever encouraged my love for writing and for all things food.

Thank you to my parents, who have continually shown their love and support for me, no matter what. I wouldn't have been able to do any of this if it weren't for them. Thank you for raising me to be strong and independent. Thank you to my mom for always being a phone call away, willing to listen to all my problems, and always there to offer great advice. Thanks to my dad for passing along the family sweet tooth and love for all things dessert! This book was partially fueled by an endless desire for anything sweet. Thanks to Andrew, my little brother, for always being willing to try anything I make. Thank you to Jared—who acted as my unofficial taste-tester, dishwasher, and grocery runner—for his endless support, patience, and encouragement.

# Index

# Notes

*Notes*